1910 ├───────┤ ├────┤ **2010**

# The
# FALL and RISE
# of
# THE EMPIRE

## Melanie Warren

An Open Mic History Books publication

First published in Great Britain in 2010
by Open Mic History Books

Open Mic History Books,
Aqueduct Road, Ewood, Blackburn BB2 4HT

A CIP catalogue record for this book
is available from the British Library.

ISBN 978-0-9563943-0-9

Printed in Great Britain by Printondemand-Worldwide

# Contents

Through a hundred years of history, the building we now know as the Thwaites Empire Theatre has hosted many different kinds of entertainment; variety, music, film, drama, and it has also been known by several names including the Red Brick Theatre, the Barn, and finally its current name which carries great local connections. In fact, the Thwaites family brewery has been connected to the theatre right from the start, because the land it was built on was owned by a Thwaites family member.

Thwaites Brewery, its fine beers now recognised all over the country and beyond, has been a mainstay of Blackburn life since its inception in 1824. It was in that year that Daniel Thwaites senior became the sole owner of the company he had joined as a partner back in 1807, and the company naturally adopted his name. His three sons inherited the Brewery after his death, with his son Daniel Thwaites II following his father's footsteps by eventually becoming sole owner. Daniel junior was a well-liked and much respected local figure, admired as a good landlord of the many pubs he owned, and he was even, for a time, Blackburn's MP.

When Daniel Thwaites II died in 1888, he left his estate to his only child; his married daughter Elma Amy Yerburgh. Elma was only 24 when she inherited, but like her father, she became well respected locally and her generosity earned her the fond nickname of 'Lady Bountiful'. She was also a good businesswoman, and it was from her that the founders of the original Empire Electric Theatre leased the piece of land on which the Theatre now stands.

**Elma Amy Yerburgh**

The lease was granted to 'Ferdinand Caton of 2 Catterall Street, Livesey Branch Road, Blackburn' and 'Christopher Hope of 191 Downham Street Blackburn'. The land concerned was an area measuring 970 square yards, bordered by the River Darwen, Bolton Road, Aqueduct Road and the then unnamed 'back road'. The lease was signed and sealed on the 14th February 1910 and the rent was set at twelve pounds, two shillings and sixpence.

Just the previous day, Ferdinand Caton and Christopher Hope had attended the Blackburn Licensing Sessions, at which their solicitor put forward an application for planning permission for a new cinema, 'costing £1,400 in Aqueduct Road, Ewood, with accommodation for 660 people on the ground floor and 222 in the gallery.' This building was, of course, the intended Empire Electric Theatre.

This application was granted, as was another for the building of the Star Cinema on Plane Street, Little Harwood and The People's Hall on King Street, but it was made very clear that any further applications for cinemas were likely to be turned down. Why? Because at that point Blackburn already boasted over a dozen cinemas!

Caton and Hope must have sighed with relief when their application was approved, because rumour has it that they had already started to build their new 'Cinematographic Hall'. Rumour also has it that the Theatre was partly constructed using timbers from Blackpool's very first Big Dipper, which is an interesting Lancastrian link. In any case, the building was built and opened for business in record time. It would have been a disaster had the Licensing Sessions turned them down!

Although Ferdinand Caton and Christopher Hope were the two original founders of the Empire, they were not the only cast members in the early history of the Empire. Within a year, their company had

Ferdinand Caton

Christopher Hope

expanded to include three more Directors: Henry Duckworth, Benjamin Meadowcroft Hall, and Henry Edward Ainsworth. As can be seen from the following potted 'family histories', none of these men had money in substantial quantity, and although some had experience of running small businesses, none had attempted such a large project before. Clearly they were men who simply had a dream – and they are to be commended for their determination, their bravery, and their cleverness at making their dream a reality.

**Ferdinand Caton** was born on the 10<sup>th</sup> of November 1856, in Lancaster. His father, John Caton, was also Lancaster-born and came from a background of extreme poverty. In 1841, according to the census, John Caton was a fatherless child of 11, living with his widowed mother and his elder sister Margaret in Damside, Lancaster. Damside was a road that ran beside the river and was arguably the poorest area of the town. But John was clearly a hard worker and by the age of 21, the 1851 census shows that he was working as a saddler – a trade of some skill. He was living with a widow, Dorothy Alston, who was also a saddler. It's probable that he was apprenticed to her and earned board and lodgings in repayment; the census describes him as Dorothy Alston's 'servant'.

Six months after the 1851 census, in September, John Caton married Sarah Greenall, Ferdinand's mother. Ferdinand was one of at least seven children. The family moved from Lancaster to Blackburn sometime in the late 1860's, where John Caton continued his trade of saddler. By 1871, three of John's daughters were working as weavers in Blackburn's cotton mills and Ferdinand, despite his young age of 14, was also working, as a clogger, making the traditional protective wooden shoes habitually worn by workers in the mills.

In 1878, when Ferdinand was 21, he married Alice Holmes. They set up home in Havelock Street, Blackburn, where they were to remain until at least 1905. They had at least seven children, many of whom grew up to follow their mother into the cotton mills.

The census of 1911 was taken six months after Ferdinand and his partner Christopher Hope won planning permission for the Empire, and shows Ferdinand and Alice and five of their grown-up children living at 2 Catterall Street, Blackburn. Ferdinand's children Thomas, Sarah and Alice were all weavers, Robert was a labourer, and Ferdinand Caton listed himself as a Managing Director.

**Christopher Hope** was born in 1860 in Blackburn, the son of Isaac Hope and Isabella Berry.

Isaac was a self-employed tradesman, making his living by the production of the metal spindles used in spinning machines. A native of Chowbent, a district of Atherton near Manchester, he moved to Preston where he married Isabella in 1857. They lived in Melling Street, Preston, where Isaac continued his trade as a spindle maker. The family, including Isabella's mother, moved to Blackburn around 1866.

The 1881 census shows that Christopher Hope and his brother William both followed their father into his trade of spindle-making, while their sisters worked in one of Blackburn's many cotton mills as winders.

Two years later, Christopher Hope married Mary Jane Dews and they had several children – the 1901 census shows the family living at 19 Coleridge Street, Blackburn, with their children Christopher, aged 16 and an iron-turner, Ethel and Isabella, 15 and 13, both cotton weavers, Eliza aged 10, Isaac aged 7, and finally Alice, aged just 1.

Sadly, baby Alice died not long after the census was taken, and Mary Jane died within a couple of years. Christopher Hope remarried in 1907; Mary Ann Moorby, who was a widow with children of her own.

By 1911, the new family was living at 191 Downham Street, Blackburn; Christopher and Mary Jane, Christopher's children Christopher, Ethel, Isabella, Eliza and Isaac, and also Thomas and Edwin Moorby, two of Mary Jane's children by her first marriage. Christopher junior was still an iron-turner and his sisters were cotton weavers, and brother Isaac was a book-keeper.

Most interesting of all is that Christopher Hope senior continued to state that his employment was 'spindle-maker' although he was by this time heavily involved in the Empire Electric Theatre, a limited company having been formed the previous September.

**Benjamin Meadowcroft Hall** was born in Heywood, Lancashire, in 1874 - and so was much younger than his business partners Caton and Hope. He was one of at least five children born to Benjamin and Hannah Hall. The 1881 census shows the family living at 4 North Side, Alice Street, Blackburn and lists Arthur Henry aged 10, William aged 8, Benjamin Hall aged 6, Martha Hannah aged 4 and Mary J., aged just 2. Two more daughters were subsequently born; Lillian, and Ada.

Benjamin Hall senior was a tripe manufacturer, but when he and his family moved to Blackburn around 1880, most of his children, including Benjamin, took work in the cotton mills, just as Ferdinand's children did. Cotton production was Blackburn's main industry at the time, so it is no surprise to find so many of the founders linked to the cotton mills in some way.

In 1895 Benjamin Hall junior married Hanna Sharples. Hanna's father Edward was a coal merchant, working 'on his own account' according to the 1891 census. This meant that he was not employed by anyone but was working for himself. For the first several years Benjamin and Hanna lived with Hanna's parents in Caroline Street, in the Mill Hill area of Blackburn, and Benjamin had clearly adopted his father-in-law's trade. By 1901 he and Hanna had two children; Edward and Elizabeth.

In the 1911 census, Benjamin and Hanna had moved to 205 Caroline Street, Mill Hill, and had just one more child, Hanna, born in 1906. Benjamin described his employment as 'Coal Merchant' and like Christopher Hope, did not mention his involvement with the Empire Electric Theatre, although he was a Director.

The Theatre had not been open for very long, so perhaps Benjamin's profit from it was still very limited, and his coal business still his main source of income. In fact, Ferdinand Caton was the only one of the five founders who mentioned his involvement at all.

**Henry Duckworth** was born in 1867 in Blackburn. He married Jane Catlow in 1890, when he was 23 and Jane 22. Henry was a 'flagger and slater'; his wife a cotton weaver, and their first home was at 18 Emma St, Livesey, Blackburn.

By 1901, Henry and Jane were living at 3 Caroline Street – like Benjamin Hall. This may be how the two men met and joined forces in the Empire Electric Theatre project.

Henry and Jane had two children – 5 year old John and 3 year old Betsy. Late in 1901 another child, Henry, was born. Sadly, Jane died early in 1903, leaving Henry with three small children to care for. He remarried before the year was out, to Lilian Bowen who was five years older than himself. They do not seem to have had any children of their own, but it must have been a relief to Henry to have a new mother for his young family.

In 1911, Henry, Lilian and the three children John, Betsy and Henry were still living in 190 Caroline St, Mill Hill. Henry was still describing himself as 'flagger and slater' and his eldest son John was his apprentice. Once again, no mention was made in the census of Henry's involvement with the Empire Electric Theatre.

**Henry Edward Ainsworth** was born in Over Darwen in 1849, to David and Sarah Ainsworth. David Ainsworth was a general labourer, but the 1861 census shows that his son Henry was a cotton weaver from a very early age – he was only 11 but already working at the mill. Henry had at least three elder brothers, as well as a younger brother and two younger sisters – seven siblings in all and possibly more.

Henry became employed in the grocery trade at the Cooperative Stores and in 1874, he married Sarah Ann Riley in Over Darwen, where they had both been born. They lived in Darwen for a while but by 1881 were living in Withnell, at 463 Bolton Road, where they would live for several years. He and Sarah had two children; 4 year old Albert and 2 year old Sarah, both born in Darwen.

Ten years later, the family was still living in Bolton Road, Withnell, and Henry described himself as 'Cooperative shopman'. Eldest son Albert, aged 14, was an assistant 'shopman' at the Cooperative, and daughter Sarah, as we might expect, was a cotton weaver, aged just 12. There were, by now, four other children; Emma aged 7, Herbert aged 6, Ethel aged 4, and Florence aged 2.

By 1901 the family had moved to the Witton area of Blackburn, living at number 1, Beverley Street. Henry was still working at the Cooperative Store but sadly his wife Sarah had died. All of his children were still living with him. The youngest, Harry, was only 8 years old. Albert, 24, had followed his father into the grocery trade, but the two eldest daughters were – as expected – working as cotton weavers.

In 1911, when Henry Ainsworth's involvement with the Empire Electric Theatre was confirmed, he and his four youngest children had moved again, to 89 New Wellington Street, in the Mill Hill area of Blackburn. Henry was 61 and retired, but did not mention his involvement with the Theatre; he described himself simply as 'ex grocery manager, cooperative'. Children Emma and Harry were also working in the grocery trade – Ethel and Florence were cotton weavers.

And so the scene is set; five men from humble backgrounds, who came together when Frederick Caton dreamed of owning his own cinema, and invited the others to join him in that dream.

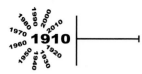
All over the country cinemas were being built in profusion and Blackburn was no different; the Empire Electric Theatre was only one of over a dozen cinemas in Blackburn early in the 20th century. Going to the cinema was regarded as a wholesome entertainment, a healthy diversion from the daily grind in a world where life was often hard. It was affordable to most people; the Empire Electric Theatre charged 3d for a seat in the stalls or 6d for a seat in the balcony.

Threepence

Sixpence

Children loved the cinema as much as adults, if not more so, finding it easy to be caught up in the action and drama on screen. Pocket-money, whether earned or given by parents, would be hoarded for cinema tickets. At a time when many families earned little more than subsistence level wages and home entertainment was virtually non-existent, going to the cinema was a small luxury which quickly became, to many, a necessity.

Despite the fact that films were, in the beginning, exclusively silent, a visit to the cinema was anything but a silent affair. Audiences would comment and shout out to the stars on screen, and of course there would be much laughter. It was very much a group experience, and often it didn't much matter what films were showing; the audiences were paying for the experience, for time in the auditorium, for relief from their daily lives.

Much as in today's cinemas, simple refreshments and drinks would be available for sale. And to keep the places hygienic, audiences remaining in their seats between films would be sprayed with sweet-smelling air-freshening liquids. (Bearing in mind that cinemas quickly earned themselves the nickname 'flea-pits', this liquid may well have been disinfectant!)

Although we believe that the Empire Electric Theatre first opened its doors in 1910, the cinema board members don't seem to have placed advertisements in the local papers until 1912; perhaps the budget wouldn't allow for this kind of expenditure in the early days. But as films moved from cinema to cinema in the town each week, we can look at the films shown elsewhere in Blackburn during 1910 and 1911, and be confident that at least some of them were also shown at the Empire.

'Up San Juan Hill' was a historical drama, telling the story of a particular battle during the Spanish-American War. The battle, which turned Colonel Theodore Roosevelt into an instant celebrity, had happened only 11 years previously and Roosevelt always referred to it as 'the greatest day of my life' – even after he became President.

'A Corner In Wheat' was a short film directed by DW Griffith. Griffith was arguably the most famous director of his day, and his work was admired as much for its artistry as for its story-telling. His best-known full-length feature film, made several years later, was 'Birth Of A Nation'.

D. W. Griffith

'A Corner In Wheat' was important enough in its own right; it is one of five DW Griffith films preserved in the US National Film Registry as being of cultural significance. It has since been described as a meditation on capitalism, although the audiences doubtless saw it only as a cracking good story. The title refers to the effect of capitalist speculators taking control of the world supply of wheat – and the effect of this on the general public as wheat prices rise and bread becomes so expensive it is quite beyond the means of the poor. Inevitably, there is a riot, and the king of the speculators meets his end suffocated under several tons of wheat.

'A Woman and Treachery' starred Theda Bara – perhaps the original 'femme fatale'. Her roles led to her nickname of 'vampire' which was

Theda Bara 1910

soon shortened to 'vamp', a term which quickly became popular slang for a sexually predatory woman. Photographs of Theda almost always show her in these characteristically 'vamp' roles, and she was undoubtedly a sex symbol. Usually her roles showed her destroying a man (or several men), and 'A Woman and Treachery' was typical, but after taking revenge on an unfaithful man, her character then fell in love with an artist and there was an unusually happy ending!

'What Happened to Brown' was a comedy, starring Johnny Butt, who is regarded as possibly the first professional English movie-actor. He is credited with roles in hundreds of films.

'His Wife's Mother' starred husband and wife team Mr & Mrs Sidney Drew. Sidney Drew was uncle to the famous Barrymore family of actors: Lionel, Ethel and John. Sidney and his wife starred in many short comedies playing a married couple in their daily lives, and as the title suggests, this one featured a mother-in-law too. A day out is planned – mother-in-law wants to visit an aquarium – the husband makes several weak excuses to absent himself, secretly planning to go to Coney Island with a friend instead. The wife is subsequently invited to Coney Island by a friend, mother-in-law goes too – and the husband's game is up.

'The Cloisters Touch', another gem from DW Griffith, was set in the Middle Ages, where a cruel Duke forces a local girl to leave her husband and baby and join his court. Clearly he has designs on her – but she is so distraught at leaving her baby that the Duke feels guilty and sends her home. Unfortunately, the girl finds that her husband's grief at losing her has caused him to take their baby and join a monastery, and she is desolate. The Duke, meanwhile, has gone to the monastery himself to confess and alleviate his guilt. His confession is heard by none other than the girl's husband! He gives the Duke forgiveness, and the family is reunited.

'The Englishman And The Girl', another short film from DW Griffith, starred Charles Craig and Mary Pickford, who was relatively new to the Griffith stable of actors, having screen-tested for him only in 1909. Her talent was immediately recognised however – she appeared in 51 films in that year alone! She was blonde, beautiful and became an instant star. 'The Englishman And the Girl' tells the story of a naive Englishman who arrives in a village to find it full of marauding Indians – unaware that they are actors in an amateur play. Finding his horror funny, some of the 'Indians' make a show of attacking him, the heroine gives him a prop gun, and he runs them out of town.

Mary Pickford 1910

'Baby's Shoe' was a melodrama produced by 'Nestor', Hollywood's first movie company. Starring Dorothy Davenport and Harold Lockwood, it tells the story of two bereaved parents whose grief is driving them apart but for whom divorce is allayed when they find their dead baby's shoes, are jointly overcome by emotion and realise they still love each other.

'The Eleventh Hour' told of a condemned prisoner about to be put to death when the governor hears that he is the prisoner's father. The governor suffers agonies of indecision about what his next move should be – but in a disappointing ending it turns out that he wasn't the prisoner's father after all. Not all those early movies were gems!

'A Brother's Devotion' was a real tear-jerker. Grieving after his mother's death, a man moves in with his younger brother who promptly steals his girlfriend. The man starts a new life in Panama whilst his brother is financially ruined by the spendthrift girlfriend. The man returns, rescues his brother from the evil girlfriend – but then dies, of yellow fever.

'Artistic Plates' was, as the title suggests, an 'interest' short film about potters. It was filmed at a ceramics factory in France and showed the entire process from mixing the clay, to shaping on a potter's wheel, through to the finished plate being painted by women. Such 'interest' films were a regular item on cinema playbills at that time; others shown that year included 'Trip to the Canary Islands', 'The Pineapple Industry' and 'Fishing in the South Sea Islands'.

### Variety acts

Let's not forget that cinemas also had live entertainment to complement the programme of films. In the beginning it was feared that watching films for extended periods might be injurious to the eyesight, so the variety acts helped to break up the proceedings.

A sample of playbills from 1910 lists at least eleven singers, four comedians, and one acrobat and an instrumentalist. More interesting acts included Tom Florence, who was a comedian and a dancer, despite having only one leg - his act was hailed as 'the greatest and most intricate clog dance in the world'! There was also Pete Rhodes the singing miner, Miss Jennie Higham the singing mill girl, and Fred Willis; 'well known eccentric character'. More exciting acts were Wee Madge; Highland fling and sword dancer, and Leonard Clarke, a boy club and sword swinger!

The first advert for the Empire Electric Cinema appeared in September 1912.

*Empire Electric Theatre Ewood*
*Grand Special Picture*
*'The Mysteries of Paris'*
*over 5,000 ft long.*
*Times and Prices as usual*

Notice the comment about the film's length – in feet, not hours and minutes! Silent films were projected at a speed of roughly 60 feet per minute, so 5,000 feet would have lasted about an hour and a quarter – quite spectacular for the times.

The images show a Bass professional 35mm cine camera, No. 1048, made in Chicago USA in 1910.

This is a wonderful, beautiful camera made from rich Honduran Mahogany. The doors are made from at least eleven separate pieces of wood. The door panels were built by the finest wood craftsmen. The look is of fine, quality cabinetry. The camera was made in the United States but the movement was licensed from a company in Prestwich, England.

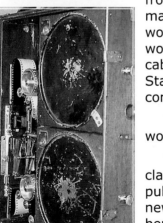

The film capacity is 400 feet, about 6 minutes worth.

'The Mysteries of Paris' was based on a classic French novel which had originally been published in parts, over a year, in a French newspaper. The novel features an aristocrat hero who dons a disguise and mixes with the lower classes, affecting several lives for the better – a murderer and a prostitute are just two of the characters who benefit from his assistance. The novel has often been cited as bearing partial responsibility for encouraging the thought-processes which inspired the French Revolution – and as such was ripe material for a movie script.

The following week, from revolutionary France to revolutionary America. . .

*Empire Electric Theatre Ewood*
*Grand Special Picture*
*'The Drummer Girl of Vicksburg'*
*An episode of the American Revolution.*

The star of this film, Anna Q Nilsson, was the first Swedish actress to become a Hollywood movie star – and the first Swede to be commemorated with a 'star' on Hollywood's Walk of Fame. She had emigrated to America as a teenager, learned English and was soon earning a living as a commercial model. She made her first film after being recommended for a role by one of the photographers employing her.

Anna Q Nilsson

As well as box advertisements, the Blackburn Times now also began to feature a Saturday review section entitled 'Places Of Amusement'. It discussed the merits of the films showing at the various cinemas in the district, and the Empire Electric Theatre was often featured, with variety acts also being mentioned alongside the films. This was doubtless very useful extra advertising. Here is the 'Review' from September 4th 1912;

*An excellent picture entertainment is provided at the Empire Electric Theatre, Ewood, this week, where large and appreciative houses have assembled. 'The Drummer Girl of Vicksburg' heads the bill, and the film is a dramatic character, depicting a thrilling episode of the American Revolution. 'Sergeants Daughter' is a fine dramatic reproduction, being over 2,000 feet in length. Other dramatic films are those of a 'Mother's Vow', 'Burglar's Reformation', 'Over the Boarder', 'Spur of the Moment'.*

*Bert Brennan is a novel instrumentalist who has proved decidedly popular. There will be a matinee today (Saturday).*

1912

In April, RMS Titanic left Southampton on her maiden voyage and sank a few days later, after hitting an iceberg.

*Next week's films include 'A Shadow Of The Past', a stirring drama, 'Over The Border, 'Reconstructed Revel', 'Shanghaied' 3,000 feet in length, 'Dad's Girls', and 'The Deception'.*

'Burglar's Reformation', mentioned in this review, starred Henry B Walthall, who was somewhat of a star at this time. He was a prolific actor, appearing in almost 50 movies in 1912 alone! Even considering the short length of most silent films, this is an active schedule. At the height of his career he earned $175 per week – an enormous sum.

The Blackburn Times of 28th September carried another glowing review of the show provided by the Empire Electric Theatre.

*There is an excellent programme presented at the Empire Electric Theatre this week, where large and appreciative houses have assembled. 'Billie' occupies the premier position on the programme, and is a dramatic portrayal of great interest. 'Lieutenant Daring Defeats the Middle Weight Champion' is also a strong dramatic film which has proved decidedly popular. 'Temporary Truce' is an exciting Western film, whilst 'Rivals' and 'Passing Shadows' are also interesting.*

Shareholders Pass from about 1912 This for Christopher Hope's Grandson

*The variety turn is provided by Wal Vordi, who is a concertina soloist and imitator of musical instruments. There will be a matinee today (Saturday).*

'Nellie the Lion Tamer' will be the principal attraction next week, and other films are entitled 'Sunset Gun', 'Home Folks', 'Baby's Woollen Shoes'. Variety turns will be provided by the Cadonna, in humour and harmony, Cullen, tenor vocalist, and Chew, baritone vocalist.

In November the following 'review' appeared;

*A varied and interesting programme is presented at the Empire Electric Theatre, Ewood, this week. 'Romance of the Coast' is a beautiful film, dealing with English life. 'On The Track of the Corkscrew Gang' is an exciting picture, over 2,800 feet in length. 'Unseen Enemy' is an*

*interesting drama, whilst 'Simple Simon', is a roaring comic. The variety turn is provided by Fred Horsfall, who has proved decidedly popular as a vocalist and mimic. There will be a matinee today (Saturday).*

Variety acts doing the rounds during 1912 were plentiful and inventive.

There were comedians; Fred Lyte, Jack Williams, Will Roscoe, Harry Royd, Jack Marsden, Jack Watson and Alf Grady. Ted E Nolan was a 'character comedian', Tom Merry was an 'eccentric character comedian', whilst Harry Herd was 'He of the smiles'. T C Jacques was 'versatile', Jack Walsh was a 'gold medal comedian', and Harry Boothman was 'the great little Harwood comedian'. Frank Whiteley was a 'comedian in song and dance' and Harry Harcourt was a 'humorist and character actor'. One advert proudly boasted the 'Expensive engagement of Alf Passmore, eccentric Dame Comedian'.

There were also comedy duos; The Nicholsons, Seymour and Mead, and Jackson and Marie – cross talk comedians.

Maude Western was a male impersonator, Vall and Derr offered 'variety specialities', Donald McBair was a Highland piper and Mr Donald Hargreaves provided 'songs and patter'. On one occasion the Empire's advert announced the 'Return visit by Alec Sherwin and his singing pictures', which conjures lovely images!

There were singers a-plenty; baritones Harry Hamer, Dick Woods, Ernest Birtwistle, Arthur Eatough, sopranos Madame St Almo, Marie Tomlinson and Miss Clara Farnworth, tenors Edward Dean, Jim Mayman, Harry Greenhalgh, and contralto Marie Earnshaw. Mollie Baldwin was 'a devote songstress with a peerless voice', and Campanello was a 'musical marvel'. Edward Harold was 'a double voiced vocalist', Squire Hughes was 'a crippled boy bass', and Pete Rhodes was a 'singing miner and actor vocalist'.

There were several duos; Ada and Ida, The Celtics, The Zetlas (Rita and Carlotta), and The Queenies. Mesdames Crampton and Bryan were, apparently, 'vocal marvels'.

For real variety, there was Schaboo, 'India's Premier Bass Vocalist', Little Eagle, 'a real Indian from the far west', and intriguingly, 'Little Paddy Keegan the Blackburn Masterpiece'! Their names spark curiosity as to the content of their acts, but sadly Little Paddy, Schaboo and the rest have long disappeared into obscurity.

Advertisements in the Blackburn Times of 1913 for films shown at the Empire offered historical and classical plays such as Ivanhoe, Dick Turpin, Mary Stuart and Uncle Tom's Cabin, many dramas and comedies, and films featuring wild animals which were very popular. Often films were announced with simple one-line descriptions such as; 'Wild Beasts at Bay – the escape from a menagerie of lions, tigers, wolves, bears etc.', 'Alone in the Jungle – thrilling animal pictures', 'Wamba, a Child of the Jungle – animal picture.'

The Cameron projector typical of the period, 1913

Sometimes films carried moral lessons, such as; 'The Call – a drama with a lesson on duplicity and revenge' and 'The Prodigal Daughter – a great picture, splendid photography and a powerful story from which much can be learned.'

Other films were listed with very short descriptions, like; 'The Red Light – plucky signalman' or 'Heroes of the Mine – drama of mining life'.

One film clearly seemed too self-explanatory as it was listed thus; 'Uphill Climb – no comment needed'!

Often, films were taken from novels, just as they are today. One of these early dramatisations was 'The Octoroon', a tale of the days of slavery in America. An 'octoroon' is a person whose ancestry was, in part, black-skinned – but who could quite possibly pass as white. The story revolves around George and Zoe who meet, fall in love, and then tragically discover that George's slave-owning father is also the father of Zoe – whose mother was a black slave. This means they cannot possibly marry, as Zoe's blackness means she is also 'property'. Finally, poor Zoe is auctioned off to help pay for debts and taxes!

'Law and Outlaw' was billed as 'a romance of the West' and starred Tom Mix, at the start of his long career. He played Dakota Joe, an atypical 'hero' who is on the run with a huge bounty on his head!

**1913**

Thousands attended the funeral of the Suffragettes' first martyr, after Emily Davidson was killed by King George V's horse at the Derby racetrack. She had run onto the racetrack as part of her protest in the fight for votes for women. Stainless steel was invented in Sheffield.

However, the crime was actually committed by his brother. He hides at a ranch and falls in love with a local beauty, Grace. Naturally, he is captured, but Grace stands by him, and visits him in his jail cell armed with a saw in a picnic basket – an early version of the 'file-in-fruitcake' escape plot. Dakota Joe breaks out of jail and uses inventive measures to escape capture, including hiding underwater and using his rifle as a breathing tube! Naturally, the film has a happy ending.

Most films were shown for only a few days, but one which showed all week was a lavish production of 'The Last Days of Pompeii', taken from Lord Lytton's famous novel. This Italian film, telling of the last few days before Vesuvius erupted disastrously in AD 79, had cost £15,000 and had also involved 2,000 actors, 5 boats, 15 lions and 50 horses.

Typical poster for the Fantomas series

One week, the Empire Electric Theatre proudly showed 'Fantomas - or the Man in Black'. This was just one of a series of very popular detective stories which were released by Gaumont. 'Fantomas' was the name of the 'hero', but he was not the detective; on the contrary, he was a master criminal who enjoyed wearing elaborate disguises to baffle the police.

Another popular series featured a more classic hero in the shape of Lieutenant Daring, all of which showed at the Empire. Stories carried titles such as 'Lieutenant Daring and the Labour Riots', 'Lieutenant Daring and the Stolen Invention', 'Lieutenant Daring avenges an insult to the Union Jack'. If the character's name were not enough, the stories' titles surely indicate that Lieutenant Daring was a thoroughly good chap!

18

In January, the Empire Electric Theatre proudly advertised that they were showing the whole of a series called 'What Happened To Mary?' Half of the entire series would be shown all together one week, and the subsequent six episodes in the week following.

Mary Fuller

This series has been called America's first serial, and comprised 12 one-reel melodramas, all based on stories previously published in the magazine 'Ladies World'. Mary Fuller played the Mary of the title. Mary is an orphan whose guardian stands to win £1,000 if he can marry her off, and the stories tell of how she escapes this fate and makes a successful life for herself – always hindered, of course, by a villain. The series made a big star of Mary Fuller, and a sequel series followed, entitled 'Who Will Marry Mary?'

'A Fight For Millions' was an action serial starring Edith Johnson as a girl forced to marry one of two distant cousins or else lose her inheritance. Of course, both cousins are entirely unsuitable and the fifteen chapters of this serial chart the heroine's tactics in avoiding the pair of them. In the end she discovers a loophole in the will and escapes her unwelcome fate.

'Adventures of Kathlyn' was yet another serial starring Kathlyn Williams as the heroine of the thirteen episodes. This was the first serial to adopt the 'cliffhanger' tactic of keeping the audience's interest, and was also the first to feature a villain who was only defeated in the last instalment. The plot was simple – pretty explorer's daughter living in India getting into scrapes with jungle animals and repeatedly rejecting the advances of a handsome native. So many different animals were used in this serial that they later became the starting-point for the collection which is now Los Angeles Zoo.

The Adventures of Kathlyn was quickly followed by others, including The Perils Of Pauline – the one where the heroine is tied to the railway line – The Exploits of Elaine, and The Adventures of Ruth.

The storyline was also released as a novel – perhaps the first 'movie tie-in' publication! And it made a star of its leading actress, the eponymous Kathlyn Williams.

As for films that were not serials; 'Kronstadt' was taken from a novel and adapted by the author himself. The orphaned heroine of the story is forced to become a Russian spy to protect the life of her younger brother.  Naturally, she is caught in the act. An officer is detailed to take her to a penal colony but the couple fall in love and she is set free. Later, she repays the officer's kindness by rescuing him from a Russian firing squad.

'From The Lion's Jaw' is set in a film studio where the heiress who supports the studio financially is rejected by a handsome actor. Hurt and angry, she releases the lions which are being used in a film – only to fall foul of the beasts herself!

'The Lighthouse Keeper' was a melodrama starring Mary Pickford and was abridged from a very famous stage play, 'Shore Acres'. Pickford plays Polly, daughter of the lighthouse keeper, who is courted by two young men who, naturally, hate each other. Mary Pickford was only 19 when she made this film but was already an accomplished actress, and this tale was perfect for her charms.

Other films during this year covered the range of subject areas. There were dramas 'The Wreck', The Live Wire' and 'The Diver' which was billed as 'a story of jealousy and intrigue'. Westerns were well represented by titles such as 'The Moonshiner's Last Stand'. Animal films remained popular, 'Within the Lion's Reach' being just one such title, and comedy continued with films such as 'Never Marry A Lawyer'.

Often films were advertised in the local newspapers with one-line descriptions, tempting readers with hints about the plot-lines;

*'Return of the Emigrant' - From Poverty to a Multi-Millionaire.*

*'Laddie' - A Scotsman away from home becomes wealthy. He is ashamed of his mother's poverty.*

*'Black Roderick' - The Lord, the Gamekeeper, His Daughter and the Poacher.*

*'The Price' - John Wakefield, in trying to meet his wife's desires, gets into financial difficulties.*

*'In The Hands of London Crooks' - This is a great film, full of sport, racing and boxing.*

Advertisements now mentioned the newsreels, which had become prominent parts of every cinema's offering. Pathe Gazette and Gaumont Graphic were examples of these. And towards the end of 1914, a new kind of newsreel began to make an appearance; 'War Pictures'.

The Pathe Illustrated Gazette was bi-weekly, in line with the usual change of cinema programmes, and through them audiences were well-informed of world events. The Gazette allowed them to witness diplomatic overtures when Lord Kitchener visited French statesman Alexandre Millerand.

They saw the Russian Army mobilised at the end of July, with officers, horses and soldiers walking past crowds of civilians, and new recruits still in civilian dress walking alongside. The crowds, in obvious high spirits, waved signs and pictures of Tzar Nicholas II, and in the background the Tzar and Tzarina appeared on a balcony.

| Lord Kitchener | Alexandre Millerand |
|---|---|

Britain declared war on Germany on August 4th.  The British people supported the decision enthusiastically, until the Battle of Mons on August 23rd demonstrated what a deadly war this promised to be.

In August, audiences saw French mobilisation in an emotively edited piece; men gathering round the doorway of an army recruitment centre, a paperboy urging 'War Declared' newspapers on passers-by, heavily-laden soldiers marching towards camera, down a street, along a country lane, a troop ship setting out from port.

Another edition continued the theme with marching French soldiers cheered on by crowds, officers on horseback carrying bouquets, hordes of soldiers waiting on railway platforms, boarding ships.

As war progressed, British troops appeared on screen, moving through a smoke screen amidst grenade explosions, then marching

French Mobilisation

through a village with the inter-title: 'After the battle some of the 'Fighting Fifth' resting. (Note their German Trophies)'. Soldiers were shown sitting on the ground, smiling, wearing German helmets, waving cheerfully at the camera.

Audiences saw captured German soldiers walking through muddy trenches; soldiers walking against a background of burned houses; English soldiers captured by German troops being led through a town. They saw an Ambulance arriving at a hospital and wounded soldiers lifted out, they saw German civilians queuing for food on the street, they saw German officers walking through a town where most buildings are reduced to rubble.

In more positive newsreels, the Gazette showed army bakers lifting loaves out of crude outdoor ovens and stacking them up whilst soldiers watched, thus proving that the troops were well-fed – and they were also entertained, as one memorable reel showing the Army's 'travelling cinema' proved. A truck bearing the legend 'Ministry Cinema' was shown, with soldiers aboard setting up projection equipment, and a crowd of eager soldiers and small boys gathering round.

Although there were over a dozen cinemas in Blackburn, their popularity ensured that even in the war years they enjoyed decent audiences, which were probably very local, and loyal. Films were shown for a few days and then passed on to other cinemas, so audiences could be sure of seeing all the most recent films, eventually.

During this, the first full year of what would become known as the Great War, it would have been unusual if the films showing at local cinemas did not reflect patriotism and public interest in the outcome, especially as there now seemed to be no end in sight. Newspaper listings for 1915 featured films such as 'The Heroine Of Mons', 'The Secret Of The Air', 'The Ordeal', and a full complement of newsreels showing scenes of action at the Front.

*January 2nd 1915*

*'The Heroine of Mons', a film illustrating incidents in the present war, has met with approval at the Empire Electric Theatre, and the management are to be complimented on its inclusion in the programme. 'Canadians Rally Round The Flag' was also exhibited, and 'In Southern Hills' was a success. A successful matinee was held on New Year's Day.*

*Next week 'The Stolen Masterpiece', described as being 'Out of the ordinary and being very interesting' will top the bill and as it is described as having a 'sound plot' it should be very popular. The film is 3,000 feet in length. A mysterious detective drama entitled 'A Speck On The Wall' will also be screened. In the latter portion of the week another portion of 'The Adventures of Kathlyn' will be depicted.*

*January 9th 1915*

*'Stolen Masterpiece', the chief film in the programme at the Empire Electric Theatre in the first portion of this week has been accorded a good reception by large houses. The film was displaced on Thursday by another showing one more of 'The Adventures of Kathlyn. '*

*'Captain Junior', a drama based on cowboy life in California, will head the bill next week.*

*Other notable films to be presented are 'The Old Cobbler', a drama, 'Pimple,' a comedy, 'Almost Human', a thrilling photo play, 'River Desperados', a 2,000 feet long exclusive, and 'In The Grip of Spies', a thrilling tale of life in the diplomatic service.*

'The Pimple', mentioned in this review, was a popular comedy, part of a long-running series written and directed by Fred and Joe Evans. Fred played 'Pimple', a character who dressed like an overgrown schoolboy with blazer and cap and face makeup resembling that of a clown. Fred and Joe Evans were descended from a long line of variety performers. Their brand of comedy relied on character and situation and often parodied other serious films and plays, including those of Shakespeare. Sometimes they were parodies of current affairs, much like the satirical sketch shows of the present day.

In February the Empire showed a drama called 'A Lancashire Lass'. This film was a tale of a mill-girl who has a remarkable singing voice, and who leaves her simple life and heads for London in search of fame and fortune. The film was especially interesting as part of it had actually been filmed in a Blackburn cotton-mill. The newspaper's review column said that *'the atmosphere of local colour is splendid'*.

Later in 1915, the newspaper review spoke particularly about a film called 'A Patriot of France or The Ordeal'. The review said; 'This picture is so realistic and depicts so truly what the invasion of this country would mean'.

The story was taken from a long poem, The Ballad Of Splendid Silence by E Nesbitt. Although the story was set in the Franco-Prussian War in 1870, it caused great consternation and controversy when it was shown in 1915. As it dealt with the defeat of France by German forces, it was seen as very anti-German. It told the story of a German general interrogating a young French soldier, who refuses to betray his country even when his own family's lives are threatened.

In the year it was shown at the Empire, a German-American pressure group took the producers to court arguing that the film was *'an unfair characterization and a misrepresentation of the German army.'* Ironically, by the time the case reached court the Germans had sunk the Lusitania, changing public opinion about the Germans irrevocably.

The following week's 'review' said *''A Patriot Of France' is a triumph of kinematography. '*

One of this year's popular serials was 'Dolly Of The Dailies', and The Empire took the opportunity to show the entire serial during one week; six parts being shown on Monday, Tuesday and Wednesday, and the last six parts following on Thursday, Friday and Saturday.

Each half of this marathon event would have lasted for an hour and a half. The story, in brief, concerns Dolly, who is invited to dinner by

1915
Farms, transport industries, engineering factories, all benefitted from more than a million women doing their part for the war effort.

Mrs Cambridge and meets Count de Rochpierre, who makes her a gift of a precious ring. Mrs Cambridge discovers a valuable necklace is missing, and then recognises Dolly's ring as her own! Even Dolly's friends begin to suspect her as a thief when another necklace is found in her house. Dolly rescues herself by talking the Count into arranging a party in his own home, where she uncovers him for the thief he really is.

And of course, throughout 1915 and until the end of the war, the Newsreels continued to be very important to the local public.

Some of the headlines for this period.

**1916**
The horrors of the Battle of the Somme took place between July and November.

The British lost 20,000 soldiers on the first day, and by November 620,000 British and French were dead, plus 450,000 Germans.

**1917**
America declared war on Germany. London was bombed by Germany for the first time.

King George V – whose real surname was the German Saxe-Coburg-Gotha – changed the name of Royal Family to Windsor.

In August, the Battle of Ypres saw many deaths at Flanders.

**1918**
The Allied forces defeated the Germans at the Battle of Amiens. In November, at 11 am on the eleventh day, an armistice came into effect and the Great War ended.

Over four years of fighting, and ten million soldiers were dead.

In Britain, the 'right to vote' was finally given to women - aged 30 or over.

Younger women would not have the vote for another ten years.

**1919**
The Irish Republican Army was formed, their aim to fight for their country's independence from Britain.

In India, Gandhi began his campaign of peaceful protest after British soldiers killed or injured around 1.500 rallying Indian nationalists.

In November, Nancy Astor became the first ever woman MP.

Jazz became popular in Britain, having been brought here by American soldiers in the war.

## 1920

Dame Agatha Christie (1890-1976) published her first detective novel, *The Mysterious Affair at Styles.*

Adolf Hitler presented his 'National Socialist' ideas in Munich.

The Unknown Warrior was buried in Westminster Abbey. He was an unidentified British soldier and the location of his death has never been revealed – his burial was intended to honour all the unknown dead of the Great War.

Throughout the year, Ireland saw riots and struggles as the IRA used violence in its fight for Irish independence – in December Martial Law was declared in an attempt to restore peace.

## 1921

January saw the introduction of car tax discs.

Winston Churchill was appointed Colonial Secretary.

Unemployment rose to over a million and the Government increased unemployment benefit.

In February French Aviator Etienne Oehmichen makes first helicopter flight.

Miners went to strike in March and coal was rationed.  The strike lasted until June.

Also in March Dr. Marie Stopes opens first family planning clinic in London.

American Astronaut John Glenn born in July.

Britain gave Ireland independence - apart from six counties in Northern Ireland which remained under British control.

Chanel No.5 perfume introduced by Coco Chanel.

First aerial cropdusting, on six-acre catalpa grove infested with leaf caterpillars, at Troy, Ohio. Two days later, found to be 99 percent effective.

"The Sheik," starring Rudolph Valentino, is released.

Diverting for a moment back to the history of the Empire Electric Theatre building, an 'agreement' dated 18th December 1922 between the Company and the Borough shows that a small piece of the land owned by the Company was gifted to the Borough. It was a tiny corner, but it enabled the Borough Council to successfully widen the main road. The Board were paid a small sum of £50 for the patch of ground.

## 1929

This year brought dramatic events to the Board of the Empire. Back in the early 1880's Blackburn Council had replaced the old narrow bridge over the River Darwen, close to the land the Empire would later occupy. The new bridge was wider, built of cast-iron and with splendid balustrades bearing likenesses of the Town's chief officials. The new bridge had been built on dry ground, and then a new watercourse was excavated, retaining walls were built on each side, and finally the river was diverted into this new passage.

In 1908 Caton and Hope had constructed the footings for the new building on the site of the old river bed. They had done this by creating a box of concrete walls six feet deep (as discovered by the Theatre Trust's excavations in 1981) which they had back-filled with steam engine ash, either from a local cotton mill or, more likely, from the nearby railway coal yard behind Ewood Park football ground.

Twenty years later, one day in 1928, Jack Duckworth, the caretaker of the Empire, noticed something odd; the eight-foot wide gate at the rear of the building seemed to have shrunk. On closer inspection, to everyone's horror, it transpired that the boundary wall was collapsing into the river! The very foundations of the Empire were in danger of collapse, because the river's retaining walls, built some fifty years before, were now so badly eroded.

Disaster loomed for the Empire. The Board could not begin to calculate the extent of the work and the cost involved in strengthening the river walls and then rebuilding those endangered parts of the building. Yet, if nothing were done, the building would surely fall down of its own accord. The responsibility, they reasoned, lay squarely at the

**1929**

Winston Churchill was now Chancellor, and in this year's budget he abolished an ancient and outdated tax on tea, which knocked a respectable four pence off the price of a pound of tea.

feet of Blackburn Corporation, and so the Board took the unprecedented step of taking the Corporation to court.

The severity of the damage to the fabric of the Empire Electric Theatre building was brought home when the Clerk to Blackburn Magistrates, Malam Brothers, inspected the building and promptly issued an order to close the balcony to the public entirely. Even so, the local residents didn't hold out much hope of the Board winning a case against the all-powerful Corporation. The Town Clerk's own sister told Harry Duckworth's wife: 'Your husband's throwing good money away, trying to fight the Corporation. He hasn't got the ghost of a chance.'

During the course of the hearing, Mr Justice Talbot and representatives of the Empire and the Corporation all put on waders and went into the river to inspect the damage personally. The fabric of the river wall was so eroded that a stick could be inserted up to 20 inches between the stones - where solid mortar should have been. To prevent further erosion a local building firm had erected a coffer-dam a few feet away from the bulging wall.

Despite everyone's misgivings, Justice Talbot found in favour of the Empire's owners, and ordered immediate restoration of the river wall by the Corporation. Furthermore, he imposed on the Corporation an obligation to maintain the wall in perpetuity. He awarded costs against the Corporation, and also substantial compensation for loss of earnings caused by the closure of the balcony and further closures whilst essential rebuilding work was carried out on the Theatre itself.

The detail of the work to be done was laid out in a document of agreement dated 21st January 1929 and it brings home with some force just how extensively the building was already damaged – and what the likely outcome might have been had this damage not been put right.

*The river bed is to be formed in accordance with the cross section and paved with six inches of concrete reinforced with three eighths of an inch diameter bars laid in eighteen inch squares. The channel in centre is to be five feet wide laid with stone setts bedded and grouted in cement. The lower portion of the old stone retaining wall shall be taken down and a reinforced concrete retaining wall shall be built – the base of the filling behind the retaining wall shall be mass concrete to a height sufficient to make secure the foundations of the Picture Theatre.*

*Upon the Concrete Retaining Wall a 9 inch brick wall stiffened with fourteen by four and one half buttresses every nine and one half feet and finished with coping set in cement as previously.*

*Rebuild the cellar steps and the retaining wall for same and reinstate the iron railing and iron gate as previously existing. Flag the rear enclosed space and the area at the bottom of cellar steps and reinstate gully and drain for same.*

*Rebuild the external wall of the emergency exit in nine inch brickwork to match the existing work and re-roof the same with timber and slates as previously. Form skylight as previously. Reinstate the cast iron gutters and downpipes and necessary drains. Reinstate the exit doors and the exit staircase. Reinstate the wood gate and fittings. Level up the surface of the ground forming side passage to Theatre and leave as formerly existing.*

*Clear away the whole of the rubbish and debris.*

It is no surprise, then, that the Empire's Board was immensely relieved at the Court's decision that all this work was to be done at the cost of the Corporation. Celebrations were certainly in order! As Harry Duckworth recalled: 'After the hearing was over, the Empire's solicitor, Mr Haworth, said: 'Let's go to the Midland for lunch'. So about ten of them did so, and got the bill made out to Blackburn Corporation. . . '

Work on the river bank from around this period. The problem with the cinema building was the bank on the other side of the bridge to the left of the picture.

This work was most probably linked to the road and bridge widening for which the small parcel of land was acquired by the Council

This year saw the start of a revolution in Blackburn cinemas, with the advent of 'talkies'. In 1926, Warner Brothers had released the first 'talking film' in the form of 'Don Juan', which used a system where sound effects and music on a wax disc were synchronised with the film

– thereby negating the need for a live orchestra or even a humble piano-player. The film was a box-office hit due to its novelty value, but it was really the film 'The Jazz Singer' that changed the popular opinion that talking films would 'never catch on'.

Warner Brothers teamed up with Western Electric to produce their 'Vita-Phone' system and the era of silent films began to move towards its close.

It is well-known that the coming of talking movies spelled the end for some silent film stars, but what is less commonly realised is how audience behaviour also had to change. Audiences of the silent films were allowed to comment loudly on films, and as others responded to those comments, audiences felt a sort of camaraderie as they watched the silents together. All that changed, of course, as talking movies came to the cinemas and audiences had to pay attention to a sound-track as well as the visual treat. Anyone making loud comments now was likely to be severely chastised!

The first Blackburn newspaper advertisement for a 'Talkie' was in February 1930, when the Grand Theatre Blackburn announced the appearance of Sybil Thorndike and John Hamilton in the '100% all talking British masterpiece 'To What Red Hell''. This was a gritty drama

1930
Englishwoman Amy Johnson, 26, flew solo from England to Australia – the first woman to do so.

in which a man kills a prostitute whilst in the grip of an epileptic seizure. He is hidden by his mother, played by Sybil Thorndike. The police assume the murder was committed by the prostitute's boyfriend, but as he is about to hang for the crime, the true killer confesses just in time.

The rest of the year saw announcements by many other cinemas that they were installing the 'latest technology' to enable them to show talking movies.

1930 Cinema Loudspeaker

In April, the Olympia Theatre offered 'Hallelujah', which the paper's reviewer described as '*a masterpiece of rhythmic sound, emotional beauty and honestly told drama. A brilliant 'Talkie' achievement, it is more than a film, it is an event. You have never seen anything like this since the introduction of the talking pictures. It is a mighty masterpiece in every sense of the world.*'

In May, the Regent advertised Pauline Frederick in 'On Trail' and Fanny Brice starring in the talking and singing picture 'My Man'.

In June, the Savoy announced the coming of 'On With The Show', which was not only a 'talkie' but was in colour! The papers described it as '*the first 100% natural colour, talking, singing, dancing picture - the most lavish and colourful picture of the season. The new colour process that was used brings out costumes, settings and players in their natural tints. It is the first all-talking, all-colour picture to be filmed, thus marking another milestone of film progress, just as the advent of Vitaphone, pioneered by Warner Bros, wrought a great change in the film industry.*'

In July, the Star Cinema closed temporarily '*for the installation of the world's best 'talkie' apparatus, the 'Western Electric' Sound System*'. This, they claimed, was the first of its kind to be installed in Blackburn. Only a few days later a local paper's reviewer announced that '*Monday*

1930

The British airship R101 crashed in France on its maiden voyage. *The Times* published its first crossword.

*will see the commencement of 'talkie' pictures at the Star with three shows daily: The opening pictures will be the famous 'Sunny Side Up', in which seven great song numbers are a feature. The Movietone Sound News will also be included in the programme.'*

In September the Majestic became a 'Talkie' theatre and its first offering starred Maurice Chevalier in 'Innocents of Paris'. From Paramount, this was a musical in which Chevalier played a cheerful push-cart singer, in Paris.

Surviving newspapers carry no indication of exactly when the Empire Electric Theatre showed its first 'talkie', but there can be little doubt that it happened around this time.

1930 - Contemporary Posters
of Maurice Chevalier

In this year the Board of the Empire decided to erect a veranda or 'lean-to' against one side of the building, to provide shelter against the weather for cinema-goers waiting for entrance to the second house. It was extensive and could shelter about 200 people who doubtless found it a useful addition to the building! The canopy survived for many decades until 1980 when it was deemed unsafe through age, and after deliberation the new owners, the Blackburn Theatre Trust, decided to demolish it.

Above. Tram passing the Empire in the 1940's The veranda is clearly visible.

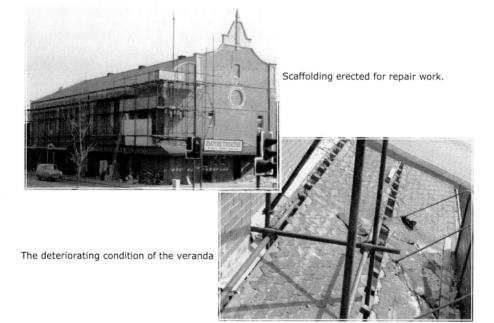

Scaffolding erected for repair work.

The deteriorating condition of the veranda

33

During the years of the Second World War, newsreels again proved themselves an important way of keeping up with current events – and naturally, many films shown at the Empire also reflected the tensions, heroisms and sacrifices of the human stories occurring in these troubled times. Two major films each week and a matinee on Thursday (half-day closing in Blackburn) kept audiences happy.

'Captains of The Clouds' had lifted its title from a phrase used by Billy Bishop, WWI fighter ace. It starred James Cagney as a Canadian pilot who does his part in the Second World War. Canada had been involved in the Second World War for over two years, whereas America had only entered the previous December, so it made sense to the American film-makers to feature Canada's ongoing efforts to encourage American patriots that this war was all for the good.

It begins as an adventure, with Cagney joining a group of bush pilots in Canada, then volunteering for service on the outbreak of war, and ends in exciting combat as Cagney leads bomber planes across the sea to England, defeating German fighter planes as he goes.

Another film, 'Unpublished Story', starred Richard Greene, famous in the 1950's as TV's 'Robin Hood'. Greene played a war correspondent working for a London newspaper. He is evacuated from Dunkirk with British troops; faces bombing raids back in London; discovers that a pacifist movement are actually Nazi supporters; and helps the British secret service save the country. He has his story – but the secret service insists it must remain unpublished... Amidst all these adventures he falls for the young reporter shadowing him (Valerie Hobson), which provides the requisite poignant romance.

One film which, whilst not featuring a war story, managed to be melancholy enough on it's own was 'H M Pulham Esq.' starring Hedy Lamarr, Robert Young and Ruth Hussey. Based on a novel by John P Marquand, and directed by King Vidor who wrote the screenplay with his wife, this was a melodrama about the sadnesses of not living life to the full.

1943
May – the 'Dambuster Raid' took place as the RAF used bouncing bombs to destroy a dam in the Ruhr valley, Germany. Sicily and Italy were invaded by the Allies, and Tunis was captured. Britain developed the Colossus computer in an attempt to break German encryption.

Robert Young played Pulham, a businessman who allows life to happen to him and never takes risks. Through flashbacks, we learn that Pulham *almost* changed his life in his early years, in order to be with Hedy Lamarr – his true love. But he settled instead for a safe and comfortable life by marrying Ruth Hussey, who plays a perfectly lovely wife, even if he doesn't love her. When Hedy Lamarr comes back into his life, Pulham is tempted to finally change his life for the better... sadly for the audiences of the day, but in keeping with 1940's morals, he denies his true feelings yet again.

Fortunately, humour and light-heartedness were not entirely absent during the war years! 'The Courtship of Andy Hardy' was the twelfth of a series of 16 films starring Mickey Rooney as the character Andy Hardy, all of which were sentimental whilst also managing to be comedies.

All the films focused on the life and times of an ordinary family in the Midwest of America. In 'The Courtship of...', Andy's father, Judge Hardy, is handling a divorce case and feels that one main issue between the couple is their daughter's intense shyness. He asks Andy to help Melodie (played by Donna Reed) settle in better with the other pupils at their school. Andy reluctantly does as he is asked and of course Melodie falls in love with him – and Andy is transformed into a better person himself.

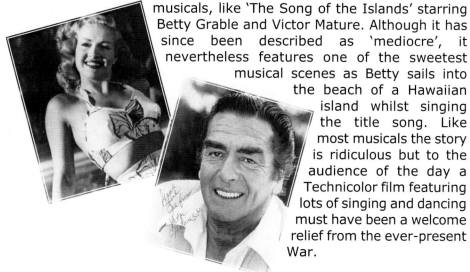

For those seeking pure escapism, there were musicals, like 'The Song of the Islands' starring Betty Grable and Victor Mature. Although it has since been described as 'mediocre', it nevertheless features one of the sweetest musical scenes as Betty sails into the beach of a Hawaiian island whilst singing the title song. Like most musicals the story is ridiculous but to the audience of the day a Technicolor film featuring lots of singing and dancing must have been a welcome relief from the ever-present War.

Betty Grable and Victor Mature

Harry Duckworth junior had taken over management of the Empire in 1942, but found it hard to combine this new responsibility with his existing job as a travelling salesman. In 1946 the decision was taken to sell the cinema to the Northern Theatre Company. This company already owned the Cinema Royal in Blackburn, and the manager, Joseph Thompson, would take care of both cinemas from now on. The company itself was based at 5 Rawson Street, in Halifax, Yorkshire, and with the addition of the Empire it now owned nine cinemas in the north of England.

The sale of the Empire, for a grand sum of £13,000, was a good decision. Television was becoming more popular every day, and would experience a further boost in popularity only a few years later, in 1953, as families rushed to buy a set in order to watch the Queen's Coronation.

The agreement to sell was signed by Benjamin Hope, Director and Jack Duckworth, Secretary and their seals affixed accordingly. And with their agreement, a new era dawned for the Empire.

The Coronation was a major, live, outside broadcast.

The Bush Model TV22 television set is typical of the sets available in 1953 and is likely to be the model on which most people watched the coronation.

The viewing screen was 9 inches!

In 1957, the Northern Theatres Company, which owned the Empire, was bought by a company known nationally to millions of cinema-goers as Essoldo.

Essoldo was a family business through and through, founded by one Solomon Sheckman. Even the name was a family matter, as Solomon coined it from letters in the names of his daughter Esther; his son Solomon; and his wife Dorothea. Es-sol-do. Solomon Sheckman was born in 1891 in Poland but came to live in Northeast England, with his parents, when he was just a boy. He first went into the cinema business around 1920, and only four years later he owned five cinemas. With his business partners, he embarked on a career of acquiring cinemas all over the country. At one point it was Britain's third largest cinema circuit.

Northern Theatres was a handy purchase for Essoldo, as it comprised eight cinemas; in Rochdale, Bury, Halifax, Dewsbury, and two each in Huddersfield and Blackburn.

The Essoldo logo from a 1955 poster and as a remnant on a building in Rotherham. Photographed in 2008.  Photo courtesy geo3pea

Films shown at the Empire, Ewood in 1969 offer a good snapshot of the popular films of the era, from drama to westerns to war films to comedy – and not forgetting the horror genre!

One well-received drama this year was 'Georgy Girl'. Lynn Redgrave played Georgina in a modern-day tale of free-living London life in the swinging sixties, with all its trials and tribulations. With a story-line reminiscent of today's soap operas, the film portrayed Georgy as a naive 22 year old who has never had a boyfriend, but who has a great relationship with her father's employer, Leamington, played by James Mason.

Georgy's life becomes complicated as her flatmate Meredith (Charlotte Rampling) becomes pregnant and has to get married. She soon falls out with her new husband Jos (Alan Bates) – and he starts an affair with Georgy. Meredith moves out, leaving her baby with Georgy and Jos – but Jos soon falls out of love and Georgy is left alone with baby Sarah.

Finally, Georgy accepts Leamington's offer of marriage because it will prevent baby Sarah being taken away from her by Social Services, giving us a happy ending of sorts.

Another tale of life in sixties London was the thriller 'Blow Up', in which David Hemmings plays a photographer who is tiring of his life, which revolves around sex, drugs and rock and roll. The film depicts the events of a single day, in which his life changes for ever as he accidentally captures a murder on film. He doesn't suspect this until later, in the darkroom, where he sets about making 'blow ups' of his photos in an attempt to solve the murder mystery.

Poster for the film from the Cannes Film Festival

A different kind of drama played out in 'Old Yeller' which was set in the 'wild west'. This was an animal story with a liberal dose of sentimentality. Old Yeller is an old stray dog (yellow like a golden Labrador) who arrives uninvited at a poor family's farm in the 1860's and causes all sorts of trouble. He has a bad reputation for stealing food and scaring animals, but he earns everyone's respect when he saves younger son Arliss from an angry bear. Elder boy Travis adopts the dog as his own, but Old Yeller meets a tragic end when he is bitten by a rabid wolf and Travis has to shoot his beloved dog to put him out of his misery.

As Travis is forced to learn important lessons about life and death, the sentimental ending comes as he is given a puppy sired by his beloved Old Yeller – christened Young Yeller in honour of his father.

On a lighter note, the comedy genre was well-represented by the famous 'Carry On' films with their cast of comic actors including Sid James, Kenneth Williams, Jim Dale, Charles Hawtrey and Joan Sims, amongst others. These films always enjoyed great popularity and often returned to cinemas time and again – in 1969 alone the Essoldo showed 'Carry On Camping', 'Carry On Up The Khyber' and 'Don't Lose Your Head' which was a 'carry on' film set in the French Revolution.

The Carry On team in 1969

| Sid James | | Peter Rogers | Gerald Thomas | Chas. Hawtrey | Hattie Jacques |
|---|---|---|---|---|---|
| | Joan Sims | | Barbara Windsor | Kenneth Williams | Jim Dale |

1969
The Beatles gave their last public performance – on the roof of the Apple studio building.

'Black Beard's Ghost' starred Peter Ustinov as Captain Blackbeard, or rather his ghost, who was condemned never to truly die after he was cursed by his last wife, a witch. In order to break the curse, Blackbeard has to do something truly good. As this is completely out of character for Blackbeard the notorious pirate, the opportunities for comedy were endless!

This year also saw the great comedy film 'Those Magnificent Men In Their Flying Machines' set in 1910 and based on an actual event when Lord Rawnsley, a British newspaper magnate, organised a Daily Post air race from London to Paris with a prize of £10,000. It starred James Robertson Justice, amongst a welter of other famous actors such as Red Skelton, Sarah Miles, James Fox, Stuart Whitman and comedians Terry Thomas and Eric Sykes.

And for comedy of a poignant nature, 'The Virgin Soldiers' offered a tale of young British soldiers, incarcerated in Singapore in 1950 and each dreaming about winning the love of the Sergeant's daughter.

War remained a popular subject, with the appearance of 'The Longest Day', Ken Annakin's film about D-Day, and 'The Guns of Navarone' featuring a host of stars – James Robertson Justice, Gregory Peck, Anthony Quinn, David Niven, Anthony Quayle and Stanley Baker. They played a team of crack-shot soldiers sent to dynamite a vital set of massive guns on a Greek island in 1943. The film is full of action, tension, double-crossing and danger, and remains a favourite to the present day.

Horror and science fiction films were increasingly popular through the sixties, as indicated by titles such as 'Plague of Zombies', 'Demons of the Swamp', 'Invitation of the Hell Creatures', 'Teenage Frankenstein' and 'I Was a Teenage Werewolf'. Christopher Lee and Peter Cushing were often to be seen in films such as 'Island Of Terror'.

Science fiction also gave us many memorable titles, including 'The Amazing Colossal Man ', 'The Body Stealers', 'It Conquered The World' and 'The Man With X-Ray Eyes', a popular science fiction film about a scientist, Dr James Xavier, and his invention of a drug which when applied to the eyes enables the user to see beyond the normal boundaries of vision. When his funding is cut off, he continues his work using himself as a guinea pig, and finds he can see through clothes and walls!

Westerns were also a favourite genre, with the release of 'Guns Of The Magnificent Seven', the third of the 'Magnificent Seven' series, and

1969
Lulu won the Eurovision Song Contest for the UK, singing 'Boom Bang a Bang.'

'Geronimo', in which Chuck Connors starred as the Apache leader who fought against the US Army for more than 20 years. The film was made in Geronimo's homeland of New Mexico and portrayed Geronimo as a hero, which he certainly was, to his own people. 'Nevada Smith', another western, starred a young Steve McQueen as a young half-Indian man, who sets out to extract revenge on the murderers of his parents.

Finally, the playbills from 1969 remind us that musicals were always popular, with Tommy Steel and Julia Foster starring in 'Half A Sixpence' with its memorable title song. Based on the 1905 novel Kipps, by HG Wells, this musical version starred Tommy Steele as Arthur Kipps, a draper's assistant who loves and loses love, comes into a fortune and loses it, and finally regains his lost love and lives happily ever after.

Cinema posters for Nevada Smith, Half a Sixpence and Geronimo

This year heralded a major change for the theatre building, as the Chairman of Essoldo reconsidered his future and that of his company. The chairman at this time was Peter Refson, the grandson of Essoldo's founder Sol Sheckman, and after years of buying and selling cinemas, he felt the time had come for him to move on. The Essoldo circuit now consisted of 52 cinemas, and Refson had decided to sell the lot, including the Empire, to a rival group of cinemas called the Classic Group - for £4.3 million. Essoldo had always prided itself on its tradition of looking after the welfare of its staff, and in keeping with this, Refson personally called each and every manager and explained Essoldo's reasoning.

There may well have been good reasons for selling up – not least the profit involved – but it spelled disaster for the 'Empire'. Quite wisely, the Classic Group examined the profitability of each and every cinema in its new acquisition. Some cinemas were bound to fall by the wayside as profit margins were judged unworkable. Under the new ownership, the 'Empire' continued to operate as a cinema for a while, but within eighteen months the Classic Group decided it was no longer a valid business and closed it down. Apart from two short periods of use as an Asian cinema, its days as an active movie-theatre were over.

## 1976

In 1976, a reprieve was nearly granted for the building which now lay empty and unused, when Classic Cinemas applied for permission to change the use of the Empire Cinema to a Bingo and Social Club. It is not known if such a licence was actually granted, but even if it were, it seems unlikely that it was ever put to good use. Within two years the fortunes of the old cinema were set to change again.

1972
Miners began a strike which lasted for seven weeks. The Gravelly Hill Interchange on the M6 opened and was quickly nicknamed Spaghetti Junction. Prince Edward, Duke of Windsor, died. *Jesus Christ Superstar* premiered in the West End, and *Mastermind* was broadcast for the first time. Access credit cards were introduced.

1976
This year saw an unprecedented long, hot summer with a heat wave causing water shortages. Princess Margaret and Lord Snowdon separated. Iceland and Britain ceased diplomatic relations over fishing rights – the dispute was christened the Cod War.

By 1978, the Empire building had lain unused for some time and was in a severely dilapidated state. Like any neglected building, the longer it lay empty, the more it deteriorated. As the year opened the damage had been exacerbated by vandals, who had broken in to the empty cinema and caused mayhem by ripping the screen and throwing black paint over it, setting off fire extinguishers, pouring paint into the electric junction box, smashing the projector and damaging several reels of film. The current manager told the press that he could not see the Classic ever opening as a cinema again. At last, the building was put up for sale, for any use or purpose.

This was interesting news for one group of people in Blackburn. The many Blackburn-based drama groups were bemoaning the recent loss of the local Community Theatre in Troy Street, which had closed down, leaving the town without a suitable venue for dramatic performances. Blackburn did not have a single theatre at that time, and although the Local Authority was talking about building a Civic Theatre, it could easily be ten years before that happened.

# Shutdown threat to Community Theatre

BLACKBURN'S Community Theatre in Troy Street, which costs nearly £10,000 a year to run is a "liability" and "unworthy of the town." And a staggering amount of money will have to be spent if the building is to continue as a theatre.

Blackburn Council would have to spend £16,800 on electrical and stage lighting equipment and structural repairs.

Mr Paul Sykes, recreation director, told the recreation committee it was not even certain that Blackburn Arts Council would want the theatre.

He said: "The arts council have only shown lukewarm interest and only three of the organisations affiliated to the council are interested in holding performances there."

Mr Sykes said that an alternative was to spend a minimum of £6,000 on making the building safe for the two basement tenants, the sea cadets and the old people's club and leasing off the theatre part of the building.

Extract from The Lancashire Evening Telegraph of 21st July 1977 outlining the problems with the Community theatre

MR SYKES

## Circus firm fined for

Several members of these drama groups now joined together and formed a new limited company called the Blackburn Theatre Trust. The sole aim of this Trust was to buy the now derelict Empire Cinema and transform it into a Theatre.

The scheme was the brainchild of Mr Peter Worden, vice-chairman of Blackburn Arts Club, and Mr Stan Tate, chairman of the Blackburn Light Operatic Society. The original group comprised eleven men and two women and the Trust was set up as a registered charity.

Peter Worden photographed in 2009

When the Trust approached the Classic Group, the response was encouraging – the price agreed was vastly reduced at only £12,000. A building survey was carried out which showed that apart from some imperative remedial work, the building was basically sound.

The Blackburn Theatre Trust felt that for a sum of around £80,000 they could turn the dilapidated cinema into a decent theatre, which could cater for the needs of the myriad local drama groups, who were currently forced to put on their productions in neighbouring villages rather than Blackburn itself.

In September of that year, the Blackburn Theatre Trust, led by Peter Worden, met with the Executive Committee of the Blackburn and District Arts Council, to ask them to consider a grant. Unfortunately, the Arts Council disagreed, feeling that any available money should be put towards the planned Civic Theatre instead.

This, of course, was not the end, by any means. Quite the reverse – history has shown it was just the beginning of a twenty-four year struggle, by a variety of indefatigable people, to provide Blackburn with a theatre of its very own.

In May of 1979, the Blackburn Theatre Trust took the first step towards their dream by completing the purchase of the Empire from Classic Cinemas. They also bought the freehold of the Empire's land from Woodfold Estates (which had been inherited by Daniel Thwaites' grandson, Lord Alvingham). The building and the land it stood on were now their property, free and clear.

Next, assistance was sought from the local press, to bring the theatre project to the attention of the local population and, hopefully, gain a lobby of support. On May 5, the following article appeared in the Lancashire Evening Telegraph.

### £1/4 MILLION PLAN FOR NEW THEATRE

*Plans are in the pipeline to open a sophisticated £250,000 theatre in Blackburn late next year, it was revealed today. The ambitious scheme will turn the vacant Empire Cinema, Ewood, into a modern centre for East Lancashire theatregoers.*

*The organisation behind the idea is Blackburn Theatre Trust Ltd, made up of people already connected with drama groups in the town. They are hoping for a generous response from the Blackburn public to help provide the cash for the theatre, which will have all the most up-to-date facilities and equipment. A number of industrialists have already shown an interest in the project and Blackburn Council are also to be approached in the fund-raising.*

*The theatre will seat more than 450 people and will also have a bar. It is hoped it will be open for Autumn 1980.*

This last estimate was optimistic, to say the least, but it showed the dedication and determination of the newly-formed Trust.

On May 8, the Lancashire Evening Telegraph ran a fuller story which included quotes from local notables. Blackburn-based actress Madge Hindle, who was at the time starring in Coronation Street, said: 'The theatre is a place where people ought to go, and if a place is good enough, people will go,' she said. 'Nothing would please me

Madge Hindle in Coronation Street 1979

more than to have my home town with a good theatre. I would enjoy going there myself. I would like to think that I might be on the stage there, some day.'

Councillor Roy Colling said: 'I think a thing like this is worthy of commendation. If people want theatre facilities there is now a group willing to provide them. I would support the idea whole-heartedly and I am sure other councillors will as well.'

Sadly, other councillors did not wholly agree with these sentiments. There was already a plan for a new Civic Theatre, and some councillors did not see a need for a second, smaller 'community' theatre. Opposing views felt that the Civic Theatre would be unlikely to be completed within ten years, and so a new community theatre was indeed a valid plan.

Objections and rebuttals continued for years to come, and naturally the local press made much of them   - but the Trust continued, undaunted, to garner local support and raise funds through a variety of innovative fund-raising events.

The first of a series of regular fund-raising meetings was held at the Saxon Inn Motor Hotel, and was attended by a healthy crowd of over a hundred people. Peter Worden, joint director of the Blackburn Theatre Trust, told the audience: 'This is no flash in the pan enterprise. There have been several ideas for a theatre in the past, but these have never come to anything. We came to realise that we must create a theatre at which the best of professional touring companies would wish to appear as well as operating as an out-station for an established repertory company. All this would be in addition to giving a home to the frustrated amateur interests of the area whose frustration has been the springboard to the project.'

At this stage the conversion plans were sketchy but the intention was clear enough - to turn the old building into a modern 450 seat

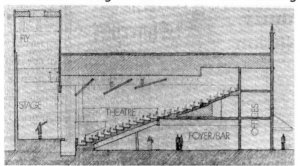

A sketch view of how the conversion could be done

theatre complete with dressing rooms, foyer bar, and the latest stage lighting equipment. The conversion would include a continuous bank of seats instead of the present stalls and balcony, and the building of a fly tower to facilitate speedy scene changes.

And at this very first public meeting, funds were given a boost by a local firm, Tom Martin Metals, whose deputy managing director, Des Roberts, donated a cheque for £3,000.

In early June vandals once again broke into the Empire and for reasons known only to themselves set about destroying whatever they could.

Blackburn Theatre Trust officials examine the seats broken by vandals in the old Empire Cinema. They are (from the left): Nigel Sharples, Peter Woods, Peter Worden and Ian Wilkinson.  Photo from the Citizen, 24 May 1979

Mystified officials found two rows of seats ripped out, light fittings destroyed, doors damaged – but in typical undaunted fashion they told news reporters: 'Luckily, we intend to completely gut the building anyway so the vandals have unintentionally set the ball rolling!'

And a few days later the Trust held another meeting, at the Spread Eagle Hotel at Mellor, and came up with some more fund-raising ideas. They would print and sell 10,000 badges emblazoned with the motto 'Let's ACT On It' – they would instigate a sponsorship scheme affordable to the man-in-the-street where the public could 'buy a seat' for £50 – and they would appeal to local businesses to donate money by Deed of Covenant, a money-making plan in which a small amount of cash invested brought substantial returns over time, worth much more than the original donation.

July saw one of the sweetest news items, featuring the efforts of two local children, Ian Swindlehurst and Victoria Livesey, who staged a show for friends and family and raised a grand total of £4.50 for the theatre appeal. Despite the small amount the Lancashire Evening Telegraph covered the story with great professionalism;

## FANGS FOR THE SHOW, KIDS

*The 'Bolton Road Kids' put on their first show last night – and it was a box-office hit. The stage-struck youngsters aged 10 and 11 put on their own version of Dracula plus a talent contest which included tap and ballet dancing and singing. The show was held in a nearby garage, and when the curtain went up there was a good audience of parents and children from the neighbourhood. The children's efforts raised £4.50 for the Blackburn Theatre Trust.*

In October, the Blackburn Theatre Trust's bid for a Council grant moved on a step, with a meeting with the Councils Finance and Performance Working Group. The Trust's application pointed out that the Trust was working hard to raise funds for a theatre which, in their opinion, would be a great asset for Blackburn. They listed over thirty organisations, all members of the Blackburn and District Arts Council, who all needed a local theatre, especially since venues such as the Odeon, the Palace and the Community Theatre had all closed in recent years. Professional touring companies had also expressed an interest in appearing at the planned theatre. And apart from being able to provide a decent space, the Empire was on a bus route and had parking facilities.

Naturally the Council were reluctant to agree to a grant immediately, although they did compliment the Trust on their 'ambitious' scheme and their dedication. They said they would need more time to come to a decision.

Several weeks later, the application was rejected. Of course, this did not much dismay the Trust, who rallied volunteers to begin clearing the interior of the cinema in preparation for the major work to be done. To pay for this work, they continued their fund-raising. Their 'Let's ACT On It!' badges had already raised £2,000 – and there was much more to come.

Blackburn Theatre Trust launched their formal Appeal in this year. As part of this effort, a number of illustrious Patrons were recruited; MPs Jack Straw, Sir Charles Fletcher-Cooke QC and Alastair Fordyce MBE, JPs Dorothy Ashworth MBE and Arnold Jepson MBE, and artist Arthur Hubert OBE FRSA.

From the world of the performing arts, Northern performers and entertainers Russell Harty, Madge Hindle, Polly James, William Roache, David Ross and Anthony Valentine all agreed to lend their names to fund-raising efforts.

Russell Harty

Madge Hindle

Anthony valentine

The Appeal's target was £150,000, which would pay for extending the stage, creating a bar, box office, foyer and disabled facilities, and building a fly tower, orchestra pit and dressing rooms. It would also pay for equipping the stage with lighting and sound systems, drapes, weights, battens, tools and ladders. To this end they applied to Blackburn Council for a loan of £200,000. The Council remained friendly but wary – they told the Trust that they needed more detailed

1980
John Lennon was shot dead by Mark Chapman as he walked into the Dakota building, where he lived with his wife Yoko Ono. He was 40 years old.

information. The Trust had made it clear that they could not guarantee they could repay a loan in full, so if in fact they were asking for a grant instead, the Council may have to reconsider.

Blackburn Theatre Trust continued to raise money through their own efforts – local businesses had already funded nearly all the exterior work. In August a fundraising leaflet was circulated to 1,200 businesses and shops, suggesting several ways they and members of the public could help – by buying a seat for £50, or by becoming a 'Friend Of The Empire' for an annual fee of £5. Another suggestion was to 'Be A Brick and Buy A Brick' for £10.

## *Blackburn Theatre Trust Appeal*

| | |
|---|---|
| **Patrons of the Trust.** | *Dorothy Ashworth M.B.E., J.P., Sir Charles Fletcher-Cooke Q.C., M.P. Alastair Fordyce M.B.E., J.P., D.L., Russell Harty, Madge Hindle, Arthur Hubert O.B.E., F.R.S.A., Polly James, Arnold Jepson M.B.E., J.P., William Roache, David Ross, Jack Straw M.P., Anthony Valentine.* |
| **Blackburn Theatre Trust Limited.** | A charitable Trust limited by guarantee (registered number 508435) is authorised to receive and administer contributions to the appeal for funds to convert and equip the theatre. The trust was formed from a group of interested enthusiasts from amateur societies within the Blackburn area who wished to create a venue for live theatre in the town. |
| **The Target . . . . We Need £150,000 for:** | - converting the interior: <br> a) extending the stage and continuing the rake from the balcony <br> b) creating bar, box office, foyer and facilities for the disabled <br> c) building a fly tower, an orchestra pit and dressing rooms <br> - equipping the stage: <br> a) lighting and sound systems <br> b) providing tabs, drapes etc. <br> c) weights, battens, tools and ladders |
| **A Theatre For Everyone.** | It is planned that the theatre when it opens in October 1982, will be available to a wide variety of users, professional and amateur alike; it will also be used as a small conference centre. |
| **Our Opportunity.** | This imaginative yet wholly practical enterprise will provide the community with a perfect small theatre capable of staging any but the largest touring shows. In addition the day long catering facilities and bar will prove an attractive meeting place for coffee and lunch. The Empire is fortunate in having a large car park adjacent to the building. |

Fundraising literature from 1980

## HOW TO HELP.

| | |
|---|---|
| **By Single Gift —** | Please make your cheques payable to 'Blackburn Theatre Trust Ltd.' |
| **By Personal Covenant —** | By spreading payments monthly, quarterly or annually over a minimum period of four years, donors of modest means can make substantial gifts. Income tax paid on gifts can be recovered by the Trust. |
| **By Company Covenant —** | For Limited Companies paying corporation tax at 52% the value of covenanted gifts to the Trust may be more than double the true cost to the company because the gross value of the covenant can be set against liability for corporation tax. |
| **By Deposited Covenant —** | Arrangements can be made for donors wishing to give a lump sum equivalent to all four or more instalments of a covenanted gift. The Appeal Director will be pleased to advise on the procedure that enables the Trust to gain immediate use of the sum deposited whilst retaining the benefits of tax recovery. |
| **By Making A Designated Gift.** | Donors may wish to associate their gifts with a particular aspect of the Theatre or its equipment. The Appeal Director will be pleased to discuss this with benefactors. |
| **Endow A Seat —** | A gift of £50 entitles the donor to 'Name A Seat'. A gift of £10 entitles the donor to 'Buy A Brick'. Leading donors will be commemorated on a plaque in the foyer. |
| **Enquiries and Contributions To:** | Mary Paul, Appeal Director, Empire Theatre, Aqueduct Road, Blackburn, Lancs. BB2 4HT. Telephone Blackburn (0254) 65566. |

Fundraising literature from 1980

Early in 1980, Ian Mackintosh from Theatre Projects Consultants Ltd in London was hired to produce a 'Strategy Report on the Provision for the Performing Arts in the Borough of Blackburn'.

The Mackintosh Report was not commissioned by the Blackburn Theatre Trust, but by the Borough of Blackburn. It reviewed the current provisions for performing arts of all kinds in the Blackburn area, and also looked at proposals which had been put forward for renovating or changing the use of six venues. Under consideration were; The Palace, The Empire, the Public Halls (King George's, Windsor, and Regency) and St John's Church.

The report discussed what kinds of live performances could currently be staged in each of the venues, how that situation might change if the venues were adapted, extended, or renovated (or, indeed, new venues built) and finally, from the viewpoint of a disinterested party, Ian Mackintosh made educated suggestions as to what actions were sensible and advisable – and which were not.

The report stated that 'a reassessment is required both of the potential of the existing buildings and of the need, if any, for new *buildings for the performing arts'*. But, it went on, three facts should be borne in mind. First, the Public Halls had already been subject to extensive examinations and estimates for necessary remedial work and also cosmetic work needed to turn this group of venues into modern usable spaces. A report five months previously had estimated the total cost at £5.2 million. The second major fact to be considered, said the Report, was the 'imaginative initiative' of Blackburn Theatre Trust in their plan to turn the old Empire cinema into a new theatre at relatively low cost. And thirdly, it should be remembered that in the midst of an economic depression, the spending of rate-payers' money must be considered carefully.

The Mackintosh Report runs to some 40 pages.

In short, it said that whilst it was 'fanciful' to suggest that Blackburn might ever have a theatre large enough to host major ballet, opera, pantomime and drama companies, it certainly did need an open stage theatre of 200 to 400 seats which would cater for medium-scale and small companies. A theatre of such a size would also be ideal for the many local amateur companies and societies.

Considering the available buildings...

The Palace – an old theatre gutted of all original theatrical features and now used as a cinema – would cost as much to convert back to a theatre as to build a brand new modern theatre. And as it was currently in full use as a cinema, the Report strongly suggested it should be left alone.

The Public Halls; firstly, King George's Hall – a report in 1979 stated 'there is consensus of opinion that this Hall has such interesting qualities that it must be preserved in its existing form.' It was without doubt a 'really excellent' concert hall but as a theatre had several short-comings in design.

Secondly, the Regency Hall was of a 'village hall design' with a flat floor and small platform stage. The 1979 report suggested that it might be partitioned to be used as office space and dressing-rooms for the adjoining Halls.

Thirdly, the Windsor Hall was simply not of the right proportions and development as a theatre.

St John's Church had the disadvantages that the County Fire Authority would demand 'rather uncompromising' alterations before it could be used as a public place – and also, the covenant of this

1980
Smallpox is considered eradicated by the World Health Organisation.

deconsecrated building forbade the sale of alcohol, wiping out the bar revenue which was valuable to most modern theatres and help them survive.

Considering the Empire, the Report described the Trust's current plans for development as 'sensible' although their costings seemed 'optimistic'. However, it was true that the remarkable enthusiasm of trust members and volunteers would result in great savings. The plans showed that the interior could be 'friendly and workmanlike', but calculations indicated that box office business would not be sufficient to meet all costs, so that fund-raising and sponsorship would be needed for the foreseeable future.

The Report summed up by saying that St John's and the Empire between them could cater for all the smaller types of performances Blackburn could expect, and so it was vital to consider them as complementary to each other, and worthy of investment and development as a pair.

Finally, the Mackintosh Report stated that the Borough of Blackburn still needed a real theatre, larger than any of the current available spaces could provide. Money should still be earmarked for such a theatre in the future.

'However,' it finished, 'nothing in the above would be wasted. King George's, the Empire and St John's would still have their part to play. Of these, only the Empire will have a conventional proscenium and stage and the protagonists of the Empire project are the first to agree that once a large, civic theatre is created, then the Empire would still have a life as a little Theatre for amateur dramas and as valuable rehearsal space.'

The Report ended by reiterating its opinion that the ideal solution was to instigate the funding for renovation of both St John's Church and the Empire into complementary spaces. 'To choose one and abandon the other,' it stated, 'would be crazy.'

The Mackintosh Report doubtless spurred the Trust on in their quest for a Theatre of their own, but in fact its findings were unlikely to sway the opinion of the Borough Council, who were already committed to finding £5.2 million for a Civic Theatre. To expect them to help fund two smaller theatres in addition was probably asking too much – but the Trust kept on asking, all the same.

In August, on the strength of the Mackintosh Report recommendations, the Trust approached the Council again, this time for a loan of just £35,000, substantially less than their original request. They had proved their worth as fund-raisers by collecting around £48,000 by their own efforts, but despite this, and despite the Mackintosh Report, their request was turned down.

Many Councillors supported the Trust's efforts wholeheartedly, and believed in their enthusiasm and ambition, but the money they needed was simply not available.

But real and practical help continued to flow from local businesses. The Trust was contacted by Jackson Steel, who offered to supply all the steel necessary to extend the theatre seating. An award scheme sponsored by Crown Paints in association with the Darwen Advertiser gave £1,000 to pay for facilities for the disabled. Benevolent Blackburn businessman Tommy Ball donated £1,000, and John Laing gave £2,000. The Gilbert & Sullivan Society announced that they were going to open a town-centre 'good as new' shop for a week, with all profits to benefit the Trust. And a major Christmas raffle was planned, with excellent prizes, which was expected to raise around £2,000.

Views from the balcony of the old cinema interior as clearance work gets under way.

Note the double or 'courting' seats fondly remembered by many past patrons.

Early in 1981 the Blackburn Theatre Trust appointed a new Appeals Director. Mary Paul's background and history as a fund-raiser made her an attractive prospect. After attending a dance and drama school, she ran a school herself for several years, and then spent time running a theatre in Bury St Edmonds, before joining Blackpool's Grand Theatre. In less than two years her efforts had boosted the Grand's appeal fund by £340,000, and hopes were high that she might do the same for the Empire.

Mary Paul April 1981

The year's first major fund-raising event took place on Sunday April 26th - a cold, grey morning which started with a blizzard. Despite bitter winds, more than 150 walkers (and one dog) took part in a sponsored walk, in aid of the Empire and the Grand Theatre in Blackpool. Friends of the Empire were bussed to the Grand to begin their thirty mile walk home, while friends of the Grand walked in the opposite direction.

There were 23 checkpoints where walkers availed themselves of refreshments - and first aid kits if necessary. 42 Blackburn walkers completed the full course, with Blackburn Theatre Trust director Kevin Miller jogging the route! Many youngsters enthusiastically took part, with teenager David Slater walking the 30 miles in six hours and 50 minutes. An American spaniel, Nuffin, completed 10 miles with owner Kathryn Warburton, sponsored at 50p per mile. Seven year old Elton Ashworth managed to complete 10 miles, while Kylie Shaw, aged only 11, completed the whole course.

The Blackburn walkers raised over £1,600 in sponsorship, meaning that the total appeal income was now in excess of £56,000.

By October, Mary Paul's efforts had boosted funds to nearly £70,000, and she announced a larger event with famous actor and author David Kossoff. In November he would entertain an audience at the Saxon Inn; a buffet supper would be included in the ticket price and later audience

members could meet David Kossoff personally as he signed copies of his books.

Pupils of Moorland High School in Darwen handed over a cheque for £50 as part of the Theatre Trust Appeal, where a seat at the Theatre would be inscribed with the school's name.

A one-day market was held by the Empire, with over 150 stalls, bargains, and fun events. And in December, actress Madge Hindle of Coronation Street picked the winning numbers at a Christmas draw at the Saxon Inn. About eighty people attended, and over £1,000 was raised.

David Kossoff

Funds continued to be boosted by events and sponsorship – in February Marks & Spencer donated the £620 needed to provide an 'induction loop'; an amplification system for the hard-of-hearing, and in April the local Gilbert & Sullivan Society donated a portion of the proceeds from their latest show.

## Store's gift to theatre

Blackburn Theatre Trust received a cheque for £620 from the Blackburn branch of Marks and Spencers in aid of installing an induction loop system in the theatre for the hard of hearing.
  Mr Philip Pickering, store manager (centre) is pictured handing over the cheque to Mr Peter Woods from the Theatre Trust, watched by Mrs Olwyn Worden. (CL8)

Article from the Citizen
18 February 1982

Society's £250 boost for theatre trust

Photo from the Lancashire Evening Telegraph 23 April 1982

By far the largest event this year was the Country Fair, organised by the Trust and held one sunny May day in nearby Witton Park. 20,000 people came along to enjoy a wide variety of traditional entertainments including Maypole dancing by local children, pony and cart rides  and a tug o' war across the river. The Balderstone Band provided music, Oswaldtwistle St Mary's Morris Dancers entertained and the Darwen Olympic Gymnastic Display Team put on a display. A market offered many stalls including a popular cake stall, and there was a fairground. And after expenses were settled, a grand total of over £3,000 was added to the appeal fund.

Later that month another two-way sponsored walk was organised, which raised another £1,200. Some 90 people took part, and 63 of them managed to walk the entire 30 miles!

In August, an unusual cycle race was held in the grounds of Hoghton Tower, where riders were timed as they tackled the two-mile uphill

1982

450 years after Henry VIII split with Rome and set up the Anglican Church, Pope John Paul II visited Britain and prayed in Canterbury Cathedral with the archbishop of Canterbury, Dr Robert Runcie. It was a major gesture of reconciliation.

journey up the drive to the Tower. The event drew international class cyclists as well as local riders - Roger Haydock of the North Lancashire Road Club made the ride on a penny farthing! More than 70 riders entered the race for prize money of £150, and afterwards a barbeque and disco was held in a marquee in the Tower grounds.

Also in August, the current Chairman, Councillor Peter Worden, stepped down from his post after four years, letting Connie Kay take his place. Miss Kay had been a director of the Trust for two years, and secretary of the Gilbert & Sullivan Society for eighteen.

Fund-raising continued. Amongst other events, television personality Richard Baker presented an evening of entertainment at the Trafalgar Hotel Samlesbury, and proceeds went to the Trust.

In November, Blackburn Theatre Trust announced to the local press that they would be staging a special Christmas pantomime, Little Red Riding Hood, in December – at Oswaldtwistle Town Hall. The cast would include popular local comedy duo Terry Barber and Stan Tate.

Terry Barber told the local newspaper: 'It is ironic that a panto being organised by a Blackburn Theatre trust should have to be staged in a

Connie Kay with the desolate interior of the old cinema.

neighbouring town, but there are no facilities for theatre in Blackburn.

This really shows the importance of the Empire Theatre Trust. There is a great need for a theatre in Blackburn. Children from local schools often have to travel as far away as Blackpool to see a pantomime during the day. If we are not careful, our children will not know what a theatre is like.'

TV personality and chat-show host Russell Harty lent his name to the Blackburn Theatre Trust in February, when he agreed to appear in an evening of entertainment at the Dunkenhalgh Hotel in Clayton le Moors.

Russell had become a patron of the Trust, and his fund-raising evening was staged as a version of his popular TV talk show, featuring

Russell in conversation with a selection of Lancashire guests, including writer and raconteur Kathleen Eyre and broadcaster Keith Macklin.

Then Russell himself took the stage to tell anecdotes about his life in television and answer questions from the audience. The evening raised around £500 for the appeal.

Russell Harty

With Russell's help, a documentary had been made about the Empire appeal and in June, the documentary 'The Empire Strikes Back' was shown for the first time to an invited audience at the Dunkenhalgh. Over £150 was raised for the appeal, and the documentary went on to be used for future fund-raising events.

The Empire's stall at Witton Park

In May, the Trust staged their second annual Country Fair at Witton Park. This year, as well as the stalls, fairground, and Balderstone Brass Band, entertainments included clog dancing, helicopter rides, and an archery display. Over £1,000 was raised.

By 1984, renovation work at the Empire came to a temporary halt. More than £75,000 had been raised for the appeal fund, but a sizeable proportion of it was in the form of covenants, which had not yet matured. Most of the available money had been spent on stripping the building's cinema interior, re-plastering, and converting the smaller rooms. But nothing more could be done within the main body of the theatre until a concrete base floor was laid, to support the rest of the auditorium. The floor had to be laid in one piece in order to give it the necessary strength to support the stage and raked seating areas. And the concrete floor would cost £50,000.

It was a time of waiting, and hoping.

The size of the task in hand. The old cinema interior almost completely cleared ready for reconstruction to begin.

A newspaper article in this year showed that nothing much had changed since 1980, when Blackburn local performance societies complained that they had to stage their productions miles from Blackburn itself.

In April, the Blackburn Amateurs followed the Blackburn Gilbert & Sullivan Society to the Civic Theatre in Oswaldtwistle. The only venue in Blackburn capable of hosting their production was King George's Hall, and as their audiences would only fill 25% of the seats, they could never hope to raise the revenue to pay for the hire-cost of the Hall.

Miss Connie Kay told the reporter that whilst the first phase of renovation of the Empire was well under way, the main hall of the theatre would not be finished for some years. Naturally, the only limitation was the amount of available cash.

The exterior of the building showing work in progress, 18 April 1986

One news article summed up the situation at the Empire in 1988, and we quote it here in full.

*Lancashire Evening Telegraph Feb 23 1988*

### Labour of Love – Eric's Empire Gets Set to Strike Back!

*If the Blackburn Trust had a fiver for every cutting on the subject in our library, it would be well on its way to getting its first show on the road.*

*A bulging packet charts the sorry tale of an unrealised dream to give Blackburn its very own live theatre in the old Empire Cinema. Nine years after the Trust took over the derelict building, it is still £100,000 and several years short of the dream coming true. But not for want of trying.*

Eric putting the finishing touches to the Box Office

*This is Eric Partington, a sort of one-man DIY band, who for the past 2 and a half years has spent Monday and Friday nights, and Saturday afternoons, restoring the building that opened in 1910 as the Empire Electric.*

*With the help of fellow trustees, Dick Peacock and Harold Carter, schoolteacher Eric has already all but complete the old foyer area, turning it into a community centre, with bar and refreshment area, toilets and central heating. Crown provided the paint but the Trust is looking for a Lord or Lady Bountiful to donate floor covering and a false ceiling to hide the steelwork in the ceiling.*

*Once that's open and making money, Eric will be able to see a chink of light at the end of the tunnel of the Trust's principal task, the restoration of the interior and its transformation into a 460 seat theatre.*

*'If you think it looks bad now, you should have seen it before. It was a bomb site', said Eric. Vandalised, flooded, a playground, doss-house and worse, it looked beyond salvation.*

*But Eric and his helpers buckled down and made it more secure, fixed the water supply, renewed the wiring, built walls, repaired brickwork. Miraculously, the seating has survived more or less intact.*

1988
The Licensing Act was changed to allow pubs to stay open from 11am to 11pm on weekdays.
The Comic Relief charity appeal was launched and the first Red Nose day raised £15 million.

*With a bit if imagination, you can visualise a small cost theatre rising one day Phoenix-like from the rubble of dereliction.*

Eric amid the rubble of the main auditorium

But when? 'The council doesn't think Blackburn needs a theatre,' said Eric, who finds it ironic that when he and fellow members of the Blackburn Gilbert and Sullivan Society put on a show, they have to go to Oswaldtwistle Town Hall. Blackburn's cavernous King George's Hall is entirely unsuitable for a small, intimate production by amateurs.

The cuttings file is dominated by Blackburn Council's refusal to back the Trust. 'If only the council would give us verbal backing, we could go ahead and apply for a grant.'

Without it, his thrice-weekly shift – 'My wife has told me to take my bed with me' – looks assured for years to come, a hand-to-mouth restoration funded by covenants, an annual pantomime and country fayre and a week's nearly-new sale.

'I hope,' said Eric, with only a suggestion of a smile, 'to see it open in my lifetime.' He is 49.

In 1992 some parts of the theatre opened for business at long last. The Trust had managed to create a pleasant rehearsal space which was being regularly used by amateur companies. The Friends of the Empire also met here regularly, and held fund-raising evenings designed to encourage young people to develop their performing skills.

However, the main auditorium was still unfinished – in fact, it could only be described as a building site.

In May the Trust hit the headlines again, resurrecting their campaign to fully convert the Empire into a working theatre. They had funded a professional 'Feasibility Study' with the purpose of using it to attract major grants. This study was a detailed analysis of what still remained to be done to convert the cinema into a centre able to host professional touring companies as well as local, amateur ones.

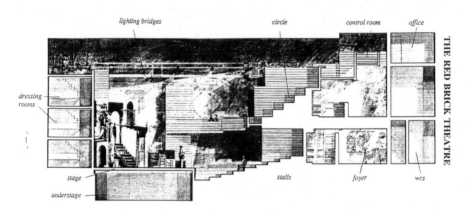

**Section of the Red Brick Theatre, Blackburn**

© Tim Ronalds Architects

Artist's impression of the conversion based on the feasibility study

The new, revised plans for the Empire advised building a timber theatre within the existing brick building, with tiered seating, lighting rig, control room and a bar.

PERFORMANCE SPACE

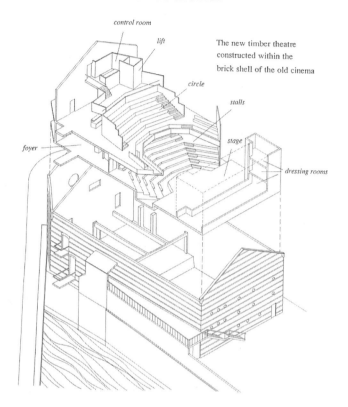

**Exploded view of the Red Brick Theatre, Blackburn**

© Tim Ronalds Architects

Architect's impression of the proposed timber theatre.

Copies of the ambitious scheme were sent to influential people including Blackburn's current MP, Jack Straw, who had long been a supporter of the Empire project. The Trust were once again appealing to the Council for grant aid, because that financial commitment was necessary before other grant agencies such as North West Arts and the ARTS Council could award grants in their turn.

Celebration! Just as the New Year arrived, Blackburn Theatre Trust was thrilled to be awarded a substantial grant by the Sports and Arts Foundation. The £25,000 grant was of enormous help in providing a concrete floor for the main auditorium of the Empire.

LANCASHIRE EVENING TELEGRAPH, Saturday, January 8, 1994    21

# £25,000 GRANT PAYS FOR FLOOR OF THEATRE

Connie Kay told reporters that the existing rehearsal room at the Empire was already well used, every night of the week and on Sundays, by Blackburn Amateurs, the Gilbert & Sullivan Society, Blackburn Disabled Arts Forum, the Friends of the Empire, Blackburn Arts Council and other local arts groups. And now, when the floor was installed, the Trust planned to build a platform at one end of the auditorium, hire seating, and apply for a temporary licence so the main theatre could, at long last, be used.

It was a real step forward.

In September, the Trust decided the time had come to find a new name for the old Empire. In a news article, they appealed to the public for ideas, suggesting that the theatre might be named after a famous northern performer or something else famous in the area. Dawson's, Weaver, and Red Brick were existing ideas.

LANCASHIRE EVENING TELEGRAPH, Saturday, September 10, 1994    5

# SUN GOING DOWN ON EMPIRE...

**New name sought for old theatre**

Headline from the Lancashire Evening Telegraph Saturday, September 10, 1994, announcing the naming appeal.

1994
The Channel Tunnel, a 51 km (31 mile) long rail tunnel beneath the English Channel, officially opened. The Church of England ordained its first female priests. Sunday trading became legal for the first time. The National Lottery was launched.

Hundreds of ideas arrived at the Empire's offices, and gradually the Trust settled on a shortlist of four: the Barn, the Phoenix, the Northern Globe and the Red Brick. All these names were appropriate, but by November, the decision had been made.

The announcement in the Lancashire Evening Telegraph
Thursday, November 17, 1994.

The old Empire Electric Theatre would henceforth be known as the Red Brick Theatre. Anyone knowing the building would agree that it was very suitable, and very descriptive of the building itself.

Towards the end of 1998, the Board of the Trust formed a new fund-raising group under the leadership of local businessman Michael Berry. A public meeting was held in October to rally support, and very soon a programme of fund-raising events was outlined. The very first event organised under Michael's leadership was a bonfire party at the Butler's Arms in Pleasington, which raised over £300.

More excitingly, an 'Open Night' was held, during which Michael Berry announced that 'Golden Tickets' were for sale – the reference to Roald Dahl's 'Charlie and the Chocolate Factory' was not so misplaced, because these were truly remarkable tickets! Costing £25, bearers would gain admission to the opening night of a show which hadn't been designed yet, on a night which couldn't be foreseen yet, in a Theatre which had yet to be built! And yet Michael sold these Golden Tickets to his audience with all the verve of a new Billy Graham – exhibiting an enthusiasm and energy which would carry the Trust forward into a new era of activity.

## 1999

1999 kicked off with the announcement of a whole series of events being held from February through to April, in aid of the theatre appeal, in the hope of reaching the target of £300,000 by May.

A Hoedown with the Quadrille Ceilidh Band at the County Hotel - Blackburn Domino Open Competition at the Railway Hotel, Pleasington - a 'Stars in Their Eyes' show featuring youngsters from the Gilbert and Sullivan Society - a concert of music from the 70's and 80's sung by local artists at the Cabin End, Knuzden - a Gala Dinner at the County Hotel, compered by Roy Walker and featuring local celebrities - a thirty mile walk from Granada Studios to the Red Brick Theatre

HAIR TODAY: A sponsored head shave was held at the Cabin End pub, Knuzden, in aid of the Red Brick Theatre Trust, Ewood , Blackburn. (From the left) are John Williams who organised the event, looking at David Holden, and Brenda Murray hairdresser from Freda's Hair Salon, Montague Street, in Blackburn

– led by a Coronation Street star - and a very special show at St George's Hall, starring the one and only Ken Dodd.

Left to right, Michael Berry, Keith Garside and Jamie Haddow

Michael Berry, Keith Garside and Jamie Haddow were the prime movers at this point, appealing to local companies to join the campaign to open the theatre. Companies prepared to be major sponsors were to be given the chance to name the theatre's various rooms, bars and studios after themselves.

In February student's from Rimmer's Technics music academy raised £125 by selling CDs of their Christmas concert – and the appeal received a major donation of £10,000 from the TDS Group, a company who made interactive whiteboards and other hi-tech equipment.

After being based in Blackburn for 25 years, the company's chairman Tony Cann said, 'I want to put something back into the town'.

TDS managing director Frank Jones (right) with Michael Berry (left), Jamie Haddow and Keith Garside.

CLASS ACT: TDS managing director Frank Jones (right) looks at plans for the Red Brick Theatre, Ewood, Blackburn. TDS has responded to a corporate appeal and pledged £10,000 to its renovation appeal. From the left, theatre appeal director Michael Berry and appeal members Jamie Haddow and Keith Garside

## The new Appeal Total now stood at £25,000.

In March, teenagers from the Gilbert and Sullivan youth section put on their 'Stars In Their Eyes' concert with impersonations of Monty Python, Frank Sinatra, Boy George and the Spice Girls, and raised more than £200. A sponsored head-shave was held at the Cabin End pub in Knuzden and a sponsored parachute jump was announced, organised by an ex-paratrooper who was offering proper training to a dozen volunteers whose only obligation was to promise £200 each in sponsorship.

March also brought an enormous step forward for the appeal as Daniel Thwaites Brewery promised financial backing to the tune of £70,000 in return for the theatre being renamed as the Thwaites Empire Theatre.

A GOLDEN OPPORTUNITY
RED BRICK THEATRE APPEAL
HELP RAISE FUNDS FOR A NEW THEATRE IN BLACKBURN

If we raise £300,000 the lottery fund will bring this up to £1 . 8 million

THIS WILL BE A THEATRE FOR EVERYBODY, SO KEEP READING.
We have 4 great events lined up that we hope you will be able to participate in, sponsor or make a donation to.

| THE RED BRICK THEATRE WALK | THE RED BRICK THEATRE CHALLENGE |
|---|---|
| Sunday 18th April 1999 | Saturday 24th April 1999 |
| Granada Studios Manchester to Ewood Theatre Blackburn | An 18 mile cross country walk that will start and finish at BURLINGTONS DINING ROOMS RIBCHESTER |
| A 21 mile walk that will have a roaring send off by a member of the cast of CORONATION STREET. Starts at 8.30 a.m. from Granada Studios. Free transport will be arranged from Blackburn and surrounding areas. A certificate for all who finish. | Parking and refreshments will be sponsored by Burlingtons Dining Rooms NIGEL EVANS M.P. for the RIBBLE VALLEY will start the walk AND TAKE PART Come and enjoy the splendours of the Ribble Valley as we cover minor roads and countryside. A certificate for all who finish. |

| Date to be Advised | Sponsored Parachute Jump |
|---|---|
| FOR THOSE WHO DARE | |
| This includes a full days training and parachute jump. On completion a Log book will be issued to prove THAT YOU DID IT (and lets you do it again). | |

| Friday 30th April 1999 | The Red Brick Theatre Walks Dinner |
|---|---|

To be held at the fabulous BURLINGTONS DINING ROOMS, RIBCHESTER.
We have reserved the restaurant for dinner guests only.
Our Guests will be NIGEL EVANS M.P. and GILLIAN GIBSON VAHE Concert Pianist.
Gillian has recently returned from Italy and we are extremely proud that she has agreed to play for us as a welcome to our guests.

Dress: Gents: Black Tie/Lounge Suit    6 Course Meal    Time: 7.15p.m. for 8.00p.m.
Ladies: Party Frocks    Tickets £23.50 each    Carriages: Midnight
Tickets are limited and are sold on the first come first served basis.

For further information on any of the above events please contact: BRIAN LEVER
Tel No. 01254 878744    Fax No. 01254 876280
or write to: Riverview, Blackburn Road, Littleton, Ribchester. Preston PR3 3ZQ

LANCER LABELS is one of the small companies of Blackburn helping to achieve this important goal. If you feel that you can help in any way please do not hesitate to make contact.

Fundraising advertising from 1999

**1999**

Prince Edward married Sophie Rhys-Jones at St George's Chapel, Windsor.

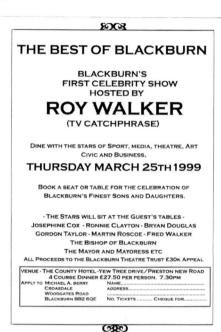

And at the end of the month, a celebrity dinner at the County Hotel, Blackburn, raised £15,000 thanks to the generosity of more than 200 guests. They were treated to a lavish dinner in the company of comedian Roy Walker, actress Madge Hindle, actor David Ross, pianist Martin Roscoe and author Josephine Cox.

Bosses of local firm S. Read and Co. pledged £5,000, more than £400 was raised through a raffle and £500 was given by an anonymous donor. Many of the celebrities also gave gifts to be auctioned at an event in June, including a mirror bearing all their signatures.

**The new Appeal Total now stood at £100,000.**

In April, the Ken Dodd show was staged at King George's Hall, featuring many local amateur acts. More than 1300 people attended the show, which raised over £5,000.

A marathon walk from Granada Studios in Manchester to Blackburn was also held this month, with walkers meeting Coronation Street Stars before they set off. And dozens of sponsored walkers, including Ribble Valley MP Nigel Evans, also completed a mammoth walk around the Ribble Valley.

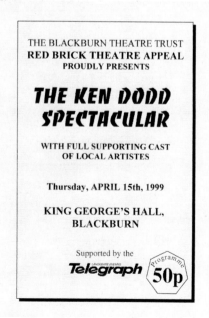

In May, accountancy firm Porter Matthews and Marsden donated £15,000 to sponsor the theatre's foyer bar, which would be renamed the PM&M Bar.

**The new Appeal Total now stood at £150,000.**

In June a marathon twelve hour show was announced, where anyone could be famous for four minutes! The marathon would need 120 performers and a newspaper article called for talented people to get in touch, whether their talent was for singing, dancing, juggling or fire-eating. Entrants would perform in heats with the winners of each heat performing against each other in the evening. Each entrant was asked to raise £20 in sponsorship money. The show took place in July and raised over £2,000! The winners were a four piece singing group, Classique.

Later in June, walkers braved teeming rain to cross the eight miles of Morecambe

**RED BRICK THEATRE APPEAL**
Blackburn Theatre Trust    Registered Charity No. 508435

**SPONSORED PERFORMATHON**

at the Red Brick Theatre, Ewood, Blackburn
to be held on SUNDAY, JULY 11th, 1999
from 9.30 a.m. to 7.30 p.m. Two acts will be selected from each two-hour Session.
FINAL at 8.00 p.m.  A cup will be presented to the best act.

NAME of Person collecting sponsorship money .............................................

ADDRESS ...........................................................................

PERFORMANCE in SESSION :        9.30 - 11.30...........;     11.30 - 1.30...........;
                          1.30 - 3.30...........;    3.30 - 5.30...........;    5.30 - 7.30...........

ACT .................................................................................

OFFICIAL accepting entry ........................... (Blackburn Theatre Trust/Fundraising Committee)

| SPONSOR'S NAME | ADDRESS | AMOUNT | INITIALS where money is paid |
|---|---|---|---|
| | | | |
| | | | |
| | | | |
| | | | |
| | | | |
| | | | |
| | | | |
| | | | |
| | | | |
| | | | |
| | | | |
| | | | |
| | | | |
| | | | |
| TOTAL OF PROMISED MONEY on this side | | | |

Sponsorship form for the Performathon

Bay and raised £680. Their efforts, along with a quiz evening, raised £680. Blackburn and District Scottish Society also donated £100 from its various fund-raising events.

In July, the Gilbert and Sullivan youth section performed five playlets and young people from the Dance Factory staged a show at St Mary's College, Shearbrow, and raised £450.

This frenetic fund-raising activity was not limited to drama groups and generous businesses. In August, a certain Marlene Devine made the newspapers with a headline of 'Running Total For Theatre' after her solo run around Witton Park raised £125.

August also saw two more rooms sponsored - WH Good Electrical Engineering Services and Pendle Frozen Foods both sponsored rooms, donating a total of £14,500.

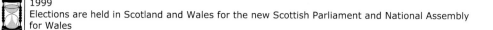
## The new Appeal Total now stood at £165,000.

**Sunday, 26th September at 7.30pm**
in the Concert Hall
The Red Brick Theatre Trust Appeal presents

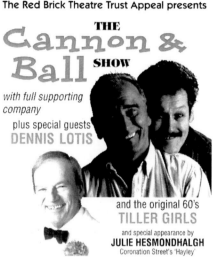

THE
**Cannon & Ball** SHOW

with full supporting company

plus special guests
DENNIS LOTIS

and the original 60's
TILLER GIRLS

and special appearance by
**JULIE HESMONDHALGH**
Coronation Street's 'Hayley'

A complete evenings entertainment with the ever-popular **Cannon & Ball**. The show also features the excellent 'Classique' and the Pat Eakets Dancers. An ideal show for all the family - and help raise much needed funds for the Red Brick Theatre!

All Seats: **£10.00**
Concessions: **£2 reduction**
Groups (of 10+): **£6.00 all seats**

**Sponsorship Opportunities**
If your organisation would like to get involved please
☎ **Steve Burch on 01254 582579**
Support of our Arts/Entertainment programme is invaluable!
PACKAGES CAN BE TAILORED TO SUIT YOUR BUDGET
★ Exclusive sponsorship of the venue, season or individual event
★ Corporate hospitality packages to entertain your chosen guests
★ Group discount rates etc, etc.
We'd be pleased to discuss your ideas/requirements

This month also saw the announcement that comedy favourites Cannon and Ball had been persuaded to host a charity variety show which would also feature other local artists such as singing group Classique, dancers and the original Sixties Tiller Girls, and veteran singer Dennis Lotis. Dennis, then 74, was very popular in the 1950's as a regular singer with the Ted Heath Band. Julie Hesmondhalgh, better known as Hayley Cropper of Coronation Street, had also promised to make a guest appearance.

Two more local firms offered financial support - Philips Components pledged to sponsor the auditorium and Barnfield Construction donated £10,000 to sponsor the theatre workshop.

In October, Blackburn Amateurs staged a production of Guys and Dolls and donated £500 to the Trust. The County Hotel hosted a literary evening where local novelist Josephine Cox spoke about her childhood memories of Blackburn and signed copies of her latest book. Other local writers gave reading and a local publisher gave a talk about getting into print – and the evening raised £400.

## The new Appeal Total now stood at £200,000.

October saw one of the most exciting fund-raising events when veteran actor Sir John Mills appeared at King George's Hall in his one-man show, talking about his long career in theatre and films and the fascinating people with whom he worked.

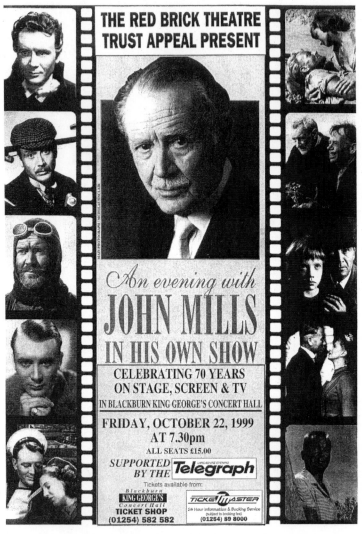

Sir John had a special fondness for East Lancashire – his wife Mary Hayley Bell wrote the novel on which the film *Whistle Down The Wind* was based, which told of three children on a Lancashire farm who help protect a runaway criminal they think is Jesus Christ. The film was made in Burnley and Clitheroe.

Organiser Michael Berry said; 'I asked him how he would like to be introduced and how he would like to come on – stage right or stage left? He said: 'I think the best thing is if I come from the right on a skateboard and shoot straight across the stage. That would make an impact!" He was 92 at the time!

The two-hour show attracted an audience of almost 500 people, and was illustrated by clips from some of his most famous films, chosen by Sir John himself. Afterwards a reception was held at Stanhill Hall, Oswaldtwistle, where guests were able to meet the man himself.

After the show, Sir John said; 'This is one of the best nights I have ever had.' And he also generously agreed to become a patron of the Theatre. He said; 'I really think it is vitally important. We are losing so many theatres. Theatres are an integral part of the community. We used to have many more touring shows than we do now. I have been in theatre for 70 years and I started my career touring England. I am a theatre man. I think it is a terrible thing to lose provincial theatre.'

The original poster from the show, signed by Sir John himself, is now proudly displayed in the Empire Theatre office.

In December, two amateur dramatic clubs, the Gilbert and Sullivan Society and Blackburn Drama Club, gave £5,000 each to the appeal, money which came from the proceeds of shows. And the youth section of the Gilbert and Sullivan Society staged another 'Stars In Their Eyes' show, adding to the theatre fund.

Michael Berry (centre) receiving pledges from Margaret Greenhalgh (left), G&S secretary, and Dorothy Perkins, of Blackburn Drama Club.

A new year dawned and the fund-raising continued apace - Des O'Connor and Sir John Gielgud lent their names to the appeal, Blackburn Chamber of Trade donated £100 of the proceeds of their annual dance, The management of Blackburn Rovers gave permission for Trust

members to organise a collection outside the ground, a 'Red Brick Rock Night' attracted over 500 music fans to hear five of the area's best bands, and three Lancashire classical tenors joined forces for a show which raised over £500.

**The new Appeal Total now stood at £200,000.**

This amazing achievement - £200,000 raised in eighteen months – did not go unnoticed. In May, the theatre's fundraiser Michael Berry was given a

Tony Parkes, Blackburn Rovers manager, with Michael Berry, Jamie Haddow and Keith Garside.

major award by the Round Table. He was nominated for their national Civic Award by the Blackburn branch for his initiative in raising money for the theatre. The Round Table's local secretary explained; 'We decided to nominate him because the appeal's been going on for twenty years and not really gathering any pace, but since Michael took it over 18 months ago, it's really taken off. There's a lot of local interest now. He's taken on a mammoth task, but he will get there.'

Michael Berry receives his award From Tom Waring (left) chairman Blackburn 83 Round Table, Eric Filpin, conference committee member and Frank Barratt, Round Table area chairman.

15 May 2000

Michael Berry was surprised – he had not even known he had been nominated - but he felt privileged to accept the award on behalf of all the volunteers, as well as a £500 cheque to add to the theatre's appeal fund.

And the fund-raising continued. TV comic Jimmy Cricket starred in 'And There's More' with a list of other artists, and a 'music hall' night was held at the Never Never Land nightclub.

July saw another major step forward with the award of £100,000 from the European Redevelopment Fund, which meant that the Trust could now afford to buy the neighbouring Reeds factory and convert it into dressing rooms and a rehearsal studio, as well as extra land to use as parking space.

**The new Appeal Total now stood at £335,000.**

So, now the magic £300,000 had been reached, was it time to stop fund-raising? Of course not!

**NAAFI NIGHT**

A Cabaret Evening devoted to the Two World Wars.
Supper of the Era will be provided.

Drinks available.

**SATURDAY SEPTEMBER 2nd**
**7.30pm**

BLACKBURN COLLEGE
FIELDEN STREET BLACKBURN

TICKET £7 inc supper

In September, Blackburn College hosted a 'Naafi Night', on the anniversary of the night before war broke out in 1939 – they served their audience with spam, seed cake and tea, and singers offered an evening of songs from both world wars.

In October, Jeff Stone hairdressers volunteered five of their staff and customers to make parachute jumps at Flukeborough, in the hope of raising £1,000 in sponsorship.

And in November, the Theatre organised a day-long experience for dozens of people who were sponsored to attempt a plane, train and boat 'pull'. The day started in Blackburn where the volunteers pulled a canal boat, 'The Kennett' (belonging to Patrick Lee, a supporter of the Theatre), along the canal to the Red Brick Theatre. Then they were taken to the Worth Valley railway to attempt to drag a steam locomotive. Next, they were bussed by Blackburn Coachlines to Manchester airport, to try their strength pulling an Airbus A321 jetliner

2000

The Queen Mother celebrated her 100th birthday. Wembley Stadium closed for three years of reconstruction.

over the tarmac. Local firm Holland's Pies provided the refreshments during the day, and later all the volunteers celebrated their successes with a bonfire night party at the Butler's Arms in Pleasington. Everyone received a commemorative T shirt and certificate.

Leeds-Liverpool canal at Waterside, Blackburn

## This massive effort raised well over £6,000.

Keighley and Worth Valley railway locomotive pull.

Air 2000 Airbus 321 at Manchester Airport and above Michael Berry with refreshments provided by Hollands Pies, 'The Pies with Pulling Power'

78

2001 was a year of renewed hard work and physical effort as the old Empire Electric Cinema was finally being transformed into a working Theatre. There was a sticky moment when the purchase of the old factory next door was almost abandoned because a promised gift of £10,000 failed to materialise – but Thwaites Brewery stepped up to the mark once again and loaned the needed cash.

The appeal total now stood at £365,000, but more cash was always needed and fund-raising events continued with a celebrity concert held at the County Hotel. Blackburn and District Arts Council also approved a small grant for £450 to pay for some speakers and a cassette rack mounted deck.

But finally, in September, the theatre was in a position to start generating income – in a small way at first – by renting out a brand new dance studio and hosting a show produced by a professional theatre company.

Volunteers worked hard at turning the new space of the former factory into space which would be usable by community groups.

Putting the final touches to the arts centre, from left to right
Harold Carter, Linda Berry, John Williams, Michael Berry, Ken Wilkinson, Eric Nolan.

This year saw the final push to see the Thwaites Empire Theatre open at last. The Blackburn Theatre Trust had a new chairman in Paul Baker, who was also managing director of Thwaites Brewery, and one of his first tasks was to announce a new campaign; 'Everyone Needs A Friend', which set out to find a team of volunteers who would be prepared to help run the Theatre when it finally opened. An army of scenery-makers, office workers, cleaners, bar staff was needed, as well as someone to sell ice-cream!

More local companies offered practical support; Pennine Fire Extinguisher Services provided all the necessary equipment needed to satisfy

Paul Baker in 2010 celebrating the 100th birthday of the Empire with a piece of birthday cake and a pint of Thwaites Smooth

regulations, CCG Limited gave toughened glass for the new box office window, and Gaskell carpets gave enough top-quality carpet to cover all the main areas in the theatre.

John Jackson (left), Pennine Fire Extinguisher Services and David Bradshaw (right), CCG managing director, with Michael Berry.

Paul Hartley of Gaskell's carpets with Michael Berry admiring one of the carpets donated by the firm

A larger worry was that a major sponsor was still needed for the arts centre attached to the Theatre, in the old factory building. Rescue came in the form of the Capita Business Centre in Blackburn, whose business director, Terry Boynes, agreed to become a sponsor, saying; 'Being involved in the theatre and sponsoring the performing arts centre is part of Capita's involvement in the community in Blackburn with Darwen. We felt that it was totally appropriate for us as an organisation to become part of the town in a real and useful way.'

And in May, at long last, the announcement came that the Thwaites Empire Theatre would open for business in October. Speaking to the local press, Michael Berry said: 'When we first started this project three and a half years ago there were people who laughed at what we were trying to achieve. But I knew from the first moment we would succeed – and we have.'

A piece of sad news came when it was announced that the County Hotel, which had hosted numerous fund-raising events for the Blackburn Theatre Trust, was to be demolished. However, the demolition proved fortunate for the Theatre, as the Trust was given permission to take anything from the building that they might find useful. Carpets, sofas, skirting boards were all willingly donated, as were entrance doors and even an entire bar!

In September, a hundred and eighty one brand new seats were installed in the theatre, meaning that the Trust could apply for a full theatre licence.

Michael Berry and Carol Barnes, Yorkshire Bank business manager, admire the new seats

Finishing touches were made to the Theatre, including new 'Thwaites Theatre' signs on the front of the building. The bar was decorated by a huge and magnificent mirror, rescued from the Vineyard Function Centre in Walton-le-Dale which had been threatened with demolition.

Eric Nolan of Blackburn Drama Club polishes the mirror rescued from the Vineyard

Michael Berry and Paul Baker, managing director of Thwaites Brewery, with the first delivery by traditional dray.

Mark Best with his painting of how the original cinema looked in the 1940's

Thwaites brewery made its first beer delivery to the theatre – by traditional horse-drawn dray. Souvenirs were available in the form of prints of a painting by local artist Mark Best, of the Theatre as it had been in the 1940's. Twenty years of hopes, dreams, fund-raising, publicity, and a fair amount of hard physical work – and finally, everything was ready.

# FROM THIS

**1979** Project begins

**1994** Digger at work

**2002** Theatre opens

# TO THIS

2002

The ex-currencies of all nations now using the Euro cease to be legal tender in the European Union.

## Saturday October 26th 2002

The Thwaites Theatre opened with a grand gala night on October 26th. Michael Berry remarked: 'Four years ago members of the public were invited to pay £25 for a ticket for the opening night, at a theatre which didn't exist, on a date which couldn't be set.' In the end, so many people wanted to attend, the opening show had to be split into two houses to accommodate everyone!

The Opening Night Show was designed as a 'sampler' of top quality shows which were booked to be staged at the Empire over the coming weeks. It featured a performance from the Gilbert & Sullivan Society, excerpts from Blackburn Drama Club's production of comedy play 'Bouncers' and the stage version of popular film 'Brassed Off', and dance from the Bernese School of Dance. A taster of 'A Night In Clubland' offered local entertainers singing the best of contemporary songs, and

Jam Factory performed some of their jazz music in league with St Wilfrid's School.

This celebratory event was staged twice; for the first house at 7.15, and for the second house at 8.45. One can only imagine the excitement and thrill that must have been felt by everyone taking part. It was a night that few thought would ever arrive – the sense of achievement felt by all concerned must have been quite overwhelming.

Post opening appeal for theatre 'Friends'

Over £400,000 had been raised to make this dream a reality – but Michael Berry and his team hadn't finished yet. The celebrations surrounding Opening Night was hardly over when a new appeal was launched, to pay for the refurbishment of the balcony area – or 'gallery' as Michael called it.

**Become a**

## ROGUE

**with**
**Ken Dodd**
**at the**
**Thwaites**
**Theatre**

The appeal invited people to become 'rogues'! Sponsors were sought to raise £1,000 each, which would pay for one seat in the 'Rogues Gallery'. The aim was to install 120 extra seats, and it was hoped the new seating would be in place by the end of 2004.

The nickname 'Rogues Gallery' also referred to an enormous framed picture which showing a theatre audience with blank faces – every person sponsoring a seat would have their photo displayed amongst this audience and it would hang in the theatre as a permanent record of all the 'rogues'.

Comedian Ken Dodd, who had previously supported the dream for a theatre in Blackburn by staging a popular amateur talent show, showed his support once more by officially becoming the Number One Rogue.

Michael Berry with the 'Rogues Gallery' where people donating funds will have their faces displayed.

2003
Mick Jagger of The Rolling Stones received a knighthood from Charles, Prince of Wales.

Less than a week after the appeal was launched, 19 people had already pledged £1,000 each and become official Rogues, amongst them three corporate names; the Bowland Theatre Trust, Thwaites Brewery and Hi-Level Maintenance.

Michael Berry told local press he was amazed by the number and variety of people who had signed up; 'They range from a twelve year old girl to pensioners.'

One of those pensioners was Betty Wilkinson, who at the age of 72 volunteered for a sponsored head-shave! She and her husband James had been involved in the theatre from the beginning. 'I plan to buy woolly hats to wear during the cold weather,' said Betty, 'and even get one with sequins on for Christmas. You've just got to go with the flow.'

**Linda's earning her place in Rogues' Gallery**

Linda Berry (left) becomes a 'Rogue' by pledging to raise £1,000 for new seats in the balcony - here holding a garden party at her home with Blackburn & Darwen Brass Band.

With Linda, from left to right, are Dave Smith, general manager of Thwaites Theatre, Justine Pursglove, Brenda Stephenson and Derek Curley.

Early in 2004, the Blackburn Theatre Trust Limited officially changed its name to the Thwaites Theatre Trust Limited.

The Trust also had a new chairman in Peter Butterfield, who as editor of the Lancashire Evening Telegraph had always been one of the Trust's greatest champions. Now retired, he launched into his new challenge enthusiastically, announcing that he planned to attempt the 'Three Peaks' walk in the Yorkshire Dales. Naturally, he invited people to join him and raise funds. 'Everyone who comes along needs to raise £1,000 for the theatre's Rogues Gallery appeal,' he said.

A long established walk, the Three Peaks was 24 miles long, involved an ascent of 5,000 feet and those completing it in 12

Peter Butterfield

hours was accepted as a member of the Three Peaks Club. However, time was not an issue. 'I don't care if it takes 15 hours so long as we raise money for the theatre,' said Mr Butterfield.

Other fund-raisers kept busy. In March, the Director of Neil Howard Telecoms offered to provide a new telephone system for the Theatre.

Howard Jones (left), managing director of Neil Howard Telecoms, with Michael Berry.

He also pledged £1,000 to join the Rogues Gallery appeal – which now had over 60 members.

Blackburn Rovers, adopted the Theatre Trust as their charity and donated £2635 from their allocation given to them by the organisers of football's Charity Shield played at Wembley every year.

Michael Berry, centre, receives the cheque from Rovers secretary Tom Finn, right, and Jim Kenyon of Lancashire FA

All 92 League Clubs get a proportion of the gate money which they can distribute to their favourite charities. The money would go towards refurbishing dressing rooms.

Encouraged by the response to the appeal, and confident that further 'rogues' would be found, the theatre arranged for final plans for the balcony – or gallery – to be drawn up.

Twenty five years had passed since the inception of the Blackburn Theatre Trust. To mark this milestone, a major 25th Anniversary Show was planned.

The show starred comedian Jim Bowen, the TV personality best-known for 'Bullseye', the game show he hosted for many years. His stage appearances were always well-received, full of stories about his life and the coincidences that led to his fame.

Local comedian Donald Banks also appeared, and singers James Loynes and Ken Nicholson. And there was a special guest appearance by Dennis Lotis.

An eight-page souvenir programme was produced for the occasion, and the back of the programme listed all the shows which were planned for the next few months – showing that the Thwaites Empire Theatre was definitely here to stay.

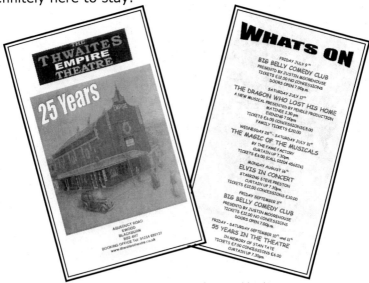

The souvenir programme front and back pages

October of this year saw the last piece of the Theatre plan falling into place as 140 brand new seats were fitted in the balcony of the Empire Theatre. The local press headline read: 'Mystery Man is Star of Theatre's Show' referring to the fact that a mystery benefactor had been responsible for the completion of this dream.

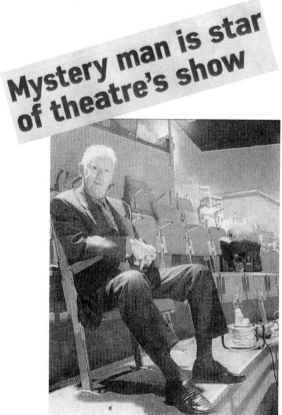

Michael Berry, project director, tries out the new seating in the balcony.

The Rogues Gallery appeal had been running successfully, with dozens of pledges of £1,000 being made by businesses and ordinary people alike – including one lady who donated her £1,000 after discussing it with her children first, as it was coming out of their inheritance!

But as Michael Berry explained: 'We had a lot of people come forward and pledge £1,000 to be a rogue but we were still £70.000 short. Thwaites Brewery, which has already done so much for the theatre, then promised a further £20,000 and out of the blue I went to see a local businessman, who gave me a cheque for £50,000 - which meant we had reached our goal. He doesn't want any publicity but it is a wonderful gesture.'

Through a myriad of selfless gestures, and through true community spirit, finally, the Theatre was complete.

In March 2007 the theatre appointed Harriet Roberts as the first full-time salaried Chief Executive of the theatre. There were many applicants for this position but it was Harriet's passion and people skills which marked her out in the eyes of Michael Berry and the board, as being the right person to take hold of the baton and raise the theatre to the next level.

Harriet Roberts

She was popular with the volunteers who were inspired to work full-time as the theatre's operational diary was very quickly pumped up to maximum capacity with bookings increased to almost every Friday, Saturday and Sunday every week.

Harriet had been a broadcast journalist at BBC Radio Lancashire during the 1990s and regularly reported on the unfolding tale of the Empire at Ewood, during a series of outside broadcasts. When she visited the theatre for her job interview, it was the first time she had seen the transformation since visiting the building site. Stepping on stage and looking out at the lovingly restored auditorium her eyes filled with tears at the remarkable accomplishment of the volunteers.

For Harriet, running a theatre had been a lifelong ambition. She had played at theatres since being a little girl, pegging up curtains in her father's garage and writing and performing plays with the children on her housing estate in the summer holidays.

After an 18 year career at the BBC, she jumped at the opportunity to apply her skills in programme making, event management, marketing and communications in a real life theatre. She had been involved in local amateur theatre as a performer and director since the age of 17, and had a network of connections across the region with societies in Burnley, Accrington, Clitheroe and Blackburn. She had even been one of the original members of the Blackburn Youth Theatre which began in 1984 and was close friends with Tim Lince, the director, and the director of Pendle Productions , a previous member of the Board of Trustees.

Harriet was given the two broad objectives of raising the profile of the theatre and increasing audiences and she attacked these with zeal.

Harriet seized the opportunity to draw on these theatre connections and with only one Gilbert & Sullivan annual musical being presented at the theatre determined to bring back to the venue the Blackburn Musical Theatre Company (originally Blackburn Amateurs) who had been performing at the nearby Oswaldtwistle Civic Theatre.

In 2008, the theatre presented an ambitious production of Fiddler on the Roof in aid of Derian House Children's Hospice. It was a collaborative project which brought together performers from societies from across East Lancashire and Manchester. It was the staging of this production that was the catalyst for other societies to realise the potential of the venue as a stage for full scale productions. Blackburn Musical Theatre Company came back to the venue and very quickly they were joined by Bacup Amateurs. In 2008 there was not one but four musicals presented in the theatre.

Many local dance schools moved from the larger local venues to the Thwaites Empire Theatre attracted by the intimacy of the space and the

Fiddler on the Roof
September 2008.

Roger Dugdale as Tevye and
Mike McKeown as Lazar Wolfe

2008
An exploding star halfway across the visible universe becomes the farthest known object ever visible to the naked eye.

cheaper venue hire cost as well as the warm welcome and friendly customer service provided by the volunteers. Schools, choirs, brass bands all began to notice the benefits of the space and very soon the diary became full.

There were other important developments that happened in a very short space of time.

New signage with the new branding.

Harriet's arrival coincided with the arrival of a new volunteer, Mike Johnson who provided the necessary skills in photography, graphic design and information technology. Together they established a new branding which replaced the red brick image. A proliferation of glossy fliers and posters succeeded in increasing audiences and with grant funding the theatre got its first online brochure, a website with full events listing, photographs, online booking facilities and links to social networking. A new telephone system with 6 lines into the building and the recruitment of new volunteers meant that the theatre could deal with the increase in bookings generated by the publicity. Flat screen televisions brought technology to audiences in the foyer bars and attracted sponsorship advertising.

A programme of daytime activities for retired people, 'The Monday Club' was established as well as a grant funded dance group for older people in partnership with Age Concern.

Working closely with Tim Lince of Pendle Productions, Harriet established a successful marketing campaign with regular sponsors for the annual pantomime. Between 2006 and 2009 box office turnover was doubled. In 2009 the income for the pantomime, Jack and The Beanstalk was £80,000 representing nearly one third of the total annual turnover for that year.

Perhaps, the most significant achievement of this period was the theatre's successful grant application to the Heritage Lottery. Harriet recognised the opportunity presented by the looming anniversary in 2010. She used her experience in community interactive learning campaigns at the BBC, to put together a proposal for a project that would enable the theatre to outreach to members of the local community and using oral history, local walks, backstage tours and a community performance enable local people to discover the history of the Thwaites Empire Theatre on their doorstep.

Supported by

# The National Lottery®
through the Heritage Lottery Fund

heritage lottery fund

A team of volunteers was recruited to piece together the piles of newspaper cuttings, ephemera and photographs that had laid dusty in boxes. They were trained to gather the memories of local people using recording equipment. With the guidance of Melanie Warren, a local history author and previously connected to Harriet at BBC Radio Lancashire, they worked together to produce this book. In June 2010 a community performance based on the history will be presented by local schools and a programme of events and activities is planned.

Andrew Schofield of North West sound Archive leading oral history training hosted by BBC Radio Lancashire

With the theatre's history in place and on the book shelf, a full bookings diary, a healthy balance sheet and a profitable trading business, Harriet turned her attention to the future. In 2010, she began work with the board of trustees in safeguarding and developing a vision for taking the theatre into a new century.

One hundred years later...

The gutted shell of the original cinema has been completely rebuilt and refurbished to provide a 330 seater auditorium with disabled access and fully tiered theatre seating. The theatre has full technical facilities for community users or visiting professional companies.

Behind the auditorium, in an adjoining modern building which was originally a factory, is the Capita Performing Arts Centre which houses rehearsal spaces, dressing rooms, a technical workshop, a professional dance studio for a resident dance school, costume and set storage facilities for a resident professional theatre company and studio facilities for a resident amateur drama club. The theatre is used as a performance venue for the following community groups:

- Blackburn and Darwen Brass Band
- Blackburn Gilbert & Sullivan Society
- Blackburn Drama Club
- Class Act - Blackburn Drama Club junior workshops
- Blackburn Musical Theatre Company
- Bernese School of Theatre, Dance & Drama
- Sandersons School of Dance
- Dancefactory
- Blackburn Youth Theatre
- Sutcliffe School of Dance
- Blackburn with Darwen Music and Arts Service
- Friends of People with Learning Disabilities
- Katrina Sudnik Dance and Drama Academy
- Blackburn India League
- Rotary Clubs, Freemasons and Charities
- Blackburn Flower Club
- Blackburn with Darwen Arts Council
- Laura James Dance School
- Bolton by Bowland Drama Group
- Little Voices
- Chantelle Leyland Dewhurst Dance Academy
- Zoe Taylor Dance School
- Lancashire Telegraph

- Porter Matthews & Marsden, accountants
- Local Primary Care Trust
- Community Health Awareness Campaigns
- Blackburn with Darwen Borough Council Performing Arts Service

In addition, the theatre runs daytime performance events and activities for older people in partnership with Age Concern. And in 2010, local schools will use the theatre as part of the 'Shakespeare for Schools' Festival.

The fact that the Thwaites Empire Theatre is now able to offer a regular performance venue and meeting place for more than two dozen performing art groups is entirely due to the tireless work of volunteers who must number, over the last thirty years, in their hundreds. The enthusiasm and ingenuity of fund-raisers is astounding. Similarly, the variety of donors, of all ages and from all walks of life, is inspiring. The £4.50 raised by two children from their own garage performance was, in its way, just a valuable as the cheque for £50.000 cheerily written out by an anonymous businessman.

Volunteers continue to play a major part in keeping the Thwaites Empire Theatre alive - from those who sell the tickets and programmes to those who work behind the bar, from cleaners to scenery-painters. All these people give their time and energy for no reward other than pride in their theatre.

Thanks are also due to the families of these many volunteers, for supporting and encouraging the efforts of all those who have worked to provide a theatre for Blackburn, despite all the odds.

The original dream, to provide a theatre for the community, has been fulfilled beyond all expectations. The Thwaites Empire Theatre is truly, and in every sense, a 'community theatre'.

# APPENDIX

## HISTORICAL DOCUMENTS

This appendix contains excerpts from historical documents relating to the history of the Empire Theatre, the land it stands on, and the original Empire Theatre Company.

### 1910 - 14th September

Mrs Yerburgh and the Trustees of the will of Daniel Thwaites deceased to Messrs Ferdinand Caton and Christopher Hope... Lease of a piece of land at the junction of Aqueduct Road and Bolton Road Blackburn for 999 years from 24 February 1910. Rent £12.2.6d.

Whitley & Co. Liverpool

Area of land 970 square yards bordered by River Darwen (100'), Bolton Road (90'), Aqueduct Road (163'6") and 'back road' (71'6").

This Indenture made the fourteenth day of September One Thousand nine hundred and ten between Elma Amy Yerburgh the wife of Robert Armstrong Yerburgh of 25 Kensington Gore London Esquire, M V William Ward of Blackburn aforesaid Esquire, Benjamin Chaffers Roberts of Oakfield Chester in the county of Chester Esquire and the said Robert Armstrong Yerburgh, hereinafter called the Lessors which expression shall include the person or persons for the time being entitled to receive the rent payable hereunder when the context so admits of the one part and **Ferdinand Caton** of 2 Catterall Street, Livesey Branch Road, Blackburn aforesaid gentleman and **Christopher Hope** of 191 Downham Street Blackburn aforesaid gentleman of the other part.

(all the land described in the plan) and also all that Hall or building with the outbuildings thereto erected on the said piece of land.

### 1910 - 28th September

Mortgage

Messrs Ferdinand Caton and Christopher Hope... To... Mr William Edmundson... Mortgage a plot of land and the building erected thereon situate at the junction of Aqueduct Road and Bolton Road Blackburn to secure £800.00 and interest.

## 1910 - 11ᵗʰ October

An agreement between Ferdinand Caton gentleman and Christopher Hope gentleman both of Blackburn (the Vendors) of the one part - and Henry Duckworth of Blackburn...

Whereas the Vendors have recently erected a Cinematograph Hall – and whereas a company is about to be formed under the Companies Consolidation Act 1908 for the purpose of acquiring and working the said Hall with a nominal capital of £2.000 divided into 200 shares of £10 each.

The Vendors shall sell and the Company shall purchase the said Hall and the land forming the site thereof and the stock and fixtures therein for all the estate and interest of the Vendors therein subject amongst other things to an indenture of Mortgage dated the 28ᵗʰ Sept 1910 between the Vendors and William Edmundson to the sum of £800 thereby secured, at the price of £1000 which shall be paid and satisfied by the allotment to the Vendors or their nominees of 100 fully paid up shares of £10 each in the Capital of the Company.

## 1910 - 28ᵗʰ November

(Assignment of the building to the Company.)

Messrs Ferdinand Caton and Christopher Hope... To... The Empire Electric Theatre (Blackburn) Limited.

Assignment of heriditaments and premises situate at the corner of Aqueduct Road and Blackburn subject to a Mortgage Debt of £800 and interest.

## 1911 - 20ᵗʰ October

Mr William Edmundson to The Empire Electric Theatre (Blackburn) Limited
Reassignment – Yates & Son, Blackburn

This Indenture made the Twenty-Eighth day of November One Thousand Nine Hundred and Ten Between Ferdinand Caton gentleman and Christopher Hope gentleman both of Blackburn (hereinafter called 'The Vendors) of the one part and The Empire

Electric Theatre (Blackburn) Limited whose registered office is situate at the corner of Aqueduct Road and Bolton Road Ewood Blackburn.

And whereas by an indenture dated the 28th day of September 1910 and made between the vendors of one part and William Edmundson of the other part the said hereditaments and premises were assigned unto the said William Edmundson his executors administrators and assigns for all the residue then unexpired of the said term of nine hundred and ninety years by way of mortgage for securing the repayment to the said William Edmundson of the principal sum of £800 and interest .

And whereas the company has been lately formed for the purpose of inter alia acquiring the said hereditaments and premises subject to the hereinbefore recited Indenture of Mortgage and by Agreement in writing dated 11th October 1910 and made between the vendors of the one part and Henry Duckworth on behalf of the Company of the other part the Vendors agreed to sell to the Company the said hereditaments and premises for the sum of one thousand pounds to be paid and satisfied by the allotment to the Vendors or their Nominees  of one hundred shares of ten pounds each ...

Was 'signed sealed and delivered' by Ferdinand Caton and Christopher Hope

And passed under the Common Seal of the Empire Electric Theatre (Blackburn) Limited in the presence of Henry Duckworth and Benjamin M Hall, Directors.


## 1911 - 21st October

Resolution passed at a Meeting of the Empire Electric Theatre (Blackburn) Limited

That the seal of the company be affixed to an Indenture dated the 21st day of October 1911 and made between this company of the first part Ferdinand Caton, clogger, Christopher Hope, Spindle and Fly Maker, Henry Duckworth, Builder, Benjamin Meadowcroft Hall, Coal Merchant,

Henry Edward Ainsworth, Secretary of a Limited Company of the second part

And William Henry Haslam of Blackburn aforesaid Licensed Victualler of the third part

Being a Mortgage of a piece of land situate in Aqueduct Road and Bolton Road Blackburn and containing 970 square yards or thereabouts and the Hall and buildings thereon for securing the payment of the sum of £700 with interest thereon at the rate of Five pounds six shillings per centum per annum.

Signed Benj. M Hall, Chairman.


## 1922 - 18th December

An Agreement between the Empire Electric Theatre Blackburn Limited and the Mayor, Aldermen and Burgesses of the Borough of Blackburn

Gifted the corner of the piece of land (in consideration of £50)

The Company hereby irrevocably dedicate to the public as part of the highway repairable by the inhabitants at large.

Signed by Ferdinand Caton and B M Hall, Directors and Fred Caton Jnr, Secretary


## 1929 - 31st January

Agreement between the Empire Electric Theatre (Blackburn) Limited And The Mayor Alderman and Burgesses of the Borough of Blackburn

The Company instituted an action in the King's Bench Division of the High Court of Justice instituted 1928 Letter E No 79 wherein the Company was the Plaintiff and the Corporation was the Defendant and thereby claimed damages for the injury sustained by the Company in respect of the land and buildings owned by it (being the Empire Electric Theatre) by reason of certain works carried out by the Corporation in the bed of the River Darwen ...

The Corporation shall forthwith proceed with and carry to completion the works in accordance with the plans signed by the Borough Engineer. Make good any damage which may have been occasioned to any part of the premises of the Company.

And the Corporation shall pay the Company the sum of £96 pounds four shillings in respect of the losses offered by the Company in the conduct of its business consequent upon the damage occasioned to its premises as aforesaid.

The Corporation shall also pay all costs.

Works to be executed-

The river bed is to be formed in accordance with the cross section and paved with six inches of concrete reinforced with three eighths of an inch diameter bars laid in eighteen inch squares. The channel in centre is to be five feet wide laid with stone setts bedded and grouted in cement. The lower portion of the old stone retaining wall shall be taken down and a reinforced concrete retaining wall shall be built – the base of the filling behind the retaining wall shall be mass concrete to a height sufficient to make secure the foundations of the Picture Theatre.

Upon the Concrete Retaining Wall a 9 inch brick wall stiffened with fourteen by four and one half buttresses every nine and one half feet and finished with coping set in cement as previously

Rebuild the cellar steps and the retaining wall for same and reinstate the iron railing and iron gate as previously existing. Flag the rear enclosed space and the area at the bottom of cellar steps and reinstate gully and drain for same. Rebuild the external wall of the emergency exit in nine inch brickwork to match the existing work and re-roof the same with timber and slates as previously.

Form skylight as previously. Reinstate the cast iron gutters and downpipes and necessary drains. Reinstate the exit doors and the exit staircase. Reinstate the wood gate and fittings. Level up the surface of the ground forming side passage to Theatre and leave as formerly existing. Clear away the whole of the rubbish and debris.

The Common Seal of the Empire Electric Theatre was affixed in the presence of Henry Duckworth, Benjamin M Hall (Directors) and Fred Caton (Secretary).


**1946 - 30th May**

Assignment between The Empire Electric Theatre (Blackburn) Limited (the vendor company And The Northern Theatres Company. Whose registered office is situate at 5 Rawson Street Halifax in Yorkshire.

Sale at the price of £13.000

Seal affixed in the presence of B Hope, Director and J Duckworth, Secretary

# ACKNOWLEDGEMENTS

This publication was produced to celebrate the centenary of the theatre in 2010, and was made possible thanks to a Heritage Lottery Grant. A team of volunteers were recruited to pull together, transcribe and scan piles of newspaper cuttings and ephemera to piece together this fascinating story so that it will never be lost or forgotten. They were led by Melanie Warren, a local author and historian.

An oral history project was also launched to collect the memories of local people, patrons, projectionists, usherettes, etc. If you can add to this story the Empire Archivist volunteers would love to hear from you via the website: www.empirearchive.net.

**With thanks to The Empire Archive Volunteers**

Lesley Blundell
Alison Carter
Martin Cottam
Bernard Kennedy
Bruce Kitchin
Marion Kitchin
Eddie Heitman

Ling Hu
Mike Johnson
Harry McGrath
Harriet Roberts
Gary Trinder
Jane Wareing

**and to the following organisations and individuals for their valued contributions**

Lancashire County Council North West Sound Archive
Lancashire Telegraph
BBC Radio Lancashire
Bruce Jackson, Lancashire County Council Archivist
Blackburn Library & Archives
Blackburn Times
The Cinema Theatre Association
Michael Berry
Linda Berry
Harold Carter
The Family of Christopher Hope
John Eatough, Napthens Solicitors
Peter Worden
Sylvia Alexander
Connie Kay
Melita Astridge